KEYLINES
FOR LIVING

Thoughts to inspire
and sustain you

Broadcast in part by Ireland's Radio 1

Ann Henning Jocelyn

Winchester, UK
Washington, USA)

First published by O Books, 2007
O Books is an imprint of John Hunt Publishing Ltd.,
The Bothy, Deershot Lodge, Park Lane, Ropley, Hants, SO24 0BE, UK
office1@o-books.net
www.o-books.net

Distribution in:

UK and Europe
Orca Book Services
orders@orcabookservices.co.uk
Tel: 01202 665432 Fax: 01202 666219 Int. code (44)

USA and Canada
NBN
custserv@nbnbooks.com
Tel: 1 800 462 6420 Fax: 1 800 338 4550

Australia and New Zealand
Brumby Books
sales@brumbybooks.com.au
Tel: 61 3 9761 5535 Fax: 61 3 9761 7095

Far East (offices in Singapore, Thailand, Hong Kong, Taiwan)
Pansing Distribution Pte Ltd
kemal@pansing.com
Tel: 65 6319 9939 Fax: 65 6462 5761

South Africa
Alternative Books
altbook@peterhyde.co.za
Tel: 021 447 5300 Fax: 021 447 1430

Text copyright Ann Henning Jocelyn 2007

Design: Stuart Davies

ISBN-13: 978 1 84694 043 9
ISBN-10: 1 84694 043 5

A CIP catalogue record for this book is available from the British Library.

Printed in Great Britain by Ashford Colour Press Ltd, Gosport, Hampshire.

KEYLINES
FOR LIVING

Thoughts to inspire
and sustain you

Broadcast in part by Ireland's Radio 1

Ann Henning Jocelyn

BOOKS

Winchester, UK
Washington, USA

CONTENTS

Birth

Have you heard about the birth myth? It is supposed to hold the key, not so much to who you are, as to who you think you are.

The birth myth is the story you've been told about circumstances surrounding your birth.

It stands to reason that it makes a difference if you were born after three days of protracted labour, so agonising that your mother vowed never to bear another child, and never did...

Or if you were the long-awaited heir hailed as a gift from heaven, whose birth was celebrated in floods of champagne; or the unwanted fruit of a shameful illicit liaison, born after a failed termination, to your mother's bitter grief.

Or perhaps you were the seventh out of ten, who slipped into the world almost unnoticed? So insignificant, even your family can't recall much about it.

Or a weakling saved against the odds amidst much tears and anguish: a triumph of life over affliction?

Often it is nothing but a myth; sometimes quite unfounded. But it still reveals a lot about your own perceptions.

Now you know what the birth myth is. The question is – what is yours?

August, 1948. A hospital in Gothenburg, Sweden. A young doctor, himself a patient, in a bare room, nearing the end of a losing battle against leukaemia.

Next to him, his wife: younger still, looking like a school-girl, except for the fact that she is nine months pregnant. They are waiting, as they have waited these last seven months, for life, for death. Which will arrive first? Will he ever see this child, their third?

The following day, she doesn't arrive as usual. Instead there is a telephone call from his colleague in the maternity unit. "Congratulations! You have a daughter."

Nobody knew where he found the strength to get up from his death-bed. He surprised them all as he entered the room, where his wife was nursing the new-born.

He took the baby in his arms, and for a short while they were together: the three of them, united by a sheer, ephemeral joy.

"Will you call her Ann?" he said, handing her back. "Ann Margareta Maria." He knew he would never see his daughter again. This was the moment he'd been holding on for.

The baptism took place the day after his funeral. They gave her the names he had requested.

Such was my entry to life, the heritage I carry. He was my father. And I was his last-born child.

I found my neighbour in tears by her cattle-shed. She looked tired and dishevelled, her clothes were stained with mud and blood.

"We lost the calf," she wept in answer to my question. "A fine bull calf. Everything was perfect. The little hooves, tail, ears; teeth and all."

Are calves born with teeth? I asked myself but I didn't say so. I sympathised with her sadness, having once shed a few tears myself over a Charolais calf, still-born for no better reason than the vet being out of reach. I remember the sight of the strong muscular body in its golden hide. The uncomprehending look of the mother as she licked him, expecting life.

My neighbour was convulsed by a sob. "Such a beautiful creature – and only fit to be buried."

I thought of her forebears: generations of women in rural Ireland, some of them still living, who gave birth to still-born children because they didn't have access to the medical services they required. Their babies were taken away in the dead of night to be buried by the men in unconsecrated ground: secret little graves, soon overgrown and forgotten.

I imagined the depth of those mothers' grief, the searing pain of loss; a nameless tragedy shared by no one. "Such beautiful creatures – and only fit to be buried."

And I wondered, would those women have wept over a calf?

The closest I have ever come to the mystery of life: a Premature Baby Unit. Watching a tiny scrap of life in intensive care struggling in agony for each breath.

Twice already he has given up and had to be resuscitated. The staff say they can do no more. The rest is up to him.

Twelve hours ago he was safe from harm. Comfortable, secure, in the warm embrace of his mother's womb. This is what he got instead. He is alone. A sign says '*No Touching*'. Each part of him is either punctured by a needle or attached to an instrument. Only his suffering cannot be treated.

"Why would he want to live?" I say to the nurse. "What attraction could life hold out to him?" She smiles. "He's getting the best possible start. From his point of view, things can only get better."

At that moment, the sun rises: a big orange on the winter horizon. A ray of hope falls on my newborn son, and suddenly, his breathing seems less laboured.

By the end of the day, he is out of danger, sleeping for the first time peacefully. Dreaming, it appears – of what? Laughing out loud – why?

In the short time he's been with us, he's known nothing but pain. Yet some secret memory is keeping him amused; giving him the courage to take on this life, knowing the suffering it contains.

So – life is a journey, a hazardous voyage of discovery; and we must negotiate our passage past adversity and trauma, undaunted like a stream rippled by jagged rocks on its steady descent to the sea.

But it's easy to lose heart; especially when you are caught in the bewildering limbo between the death of the old and the birth of the new.

That's when we have to remember Phoenix, who rose, time and again, from the ashes of the past. Take comfort from the knowledge that we have bypassed the greatest peril of all: that of stagnation.

The ancients looked on each crisis as a blessing: a liberation, the enforced breaking of new ground. Favourable to them was anything that helped our progress from darkness to light.

There are even those who claim that extraordinary afflictions are not the punishment for extraordinary sins but the trial of extraordinary graces bestowed on a favoured few.

Looking back, you may well agree that some of your worst experiences did in fact carry within them the seed of something good.

Relish the shadows you leave behind. They add depth and definition. For expansion, though, look forward: into the dazzling new dimension of the unknown.

You'll see that there are no endings in life. Only beginnings.

Childhood

What were you like as a child? Serious, responsible? Happy-go-lucky? Sweet-natured? Hyperactive? A playground bully? Or a timid creature clinging to your mother's skirt?

I spent my childhood as a fly on the wall: looking, listening, taking in impressions of the world around me: some awesome, reassuring: warmth and kindness, glimpses of pure joy; others worrying, confounding: falsehood and pretensions, spite, aggression, scorn.

Uncertain what to make of it all, I kept my observations and reflections strictly to myself.

Today I'm still the same fly on the wall, though somewhat less bemused, having taken on board some vital lessons of sympathy and compassion, tolerance and forgiveness.

Also, over the years I have acquired enough confidence to articulate my thoughts and, at length, summoned the courage to share them this way.

We're tempted to change as we grow older, in response to adult pressures: roles we are expected to perform, personally, professionally; standards set by our contemporaries, not forgetting a natural desire to develop and mature.

But our basic disposition remains the same. And rather than distance ourselves from what we were as children, we should take good care of our original equipment.

As long as it's put to good use, there will always be room for it in the adult world.

Early memories can be deceptive, in that they are usually quite appealing. As if, in the whole range of emotions experienced by a young child, pleasure is the main one to register.

This innocent, infantile inclination to acknowledge only the positive may be a protective mechanism designed to build up our morale as a bulwark against difficulties ahead.

Or else these impressions are part of a myth created by ourselves, saying more about us than about our childhood.

Even so – they have to emanate from somewhere. I'd say that's enough to justify them.

I recall – or believe that I recall – lying in my pram, being wheeled through a forest, watching high above the sun-lit tops of giant fir-trees standing out deep green against a clear blue sky dotted with cotton-wool clouds. Birds are singing, brooks are babbling, the air has the fresh smell of earth and conifers.

Closer to, my mother's face: her eyes sad, lost in the distance. I call out to her, and she smiles. I smile back. Now we are both happy.

And I have a cosy recollection of her in middle of the night, coming to lift me out of my cot, taking me to her bed, where we curl up together. I go back to sleep in her soft warm embrace, clutched by her like a teddy bear.

Giving comfort, though I know nothing about grief. Have no way of comprehending the meaning of despair.

"But I had a happy childhood!" protested the man, to whom I'd tactfully suggested that his chronic health problems might be somehow related to the traumas I knew had overshadowed his early years.

We were close enough for me to gently challenge his assertion: "But with your mother dying so early… And not having a father… That must have been difficult."

"Oh I don't know… I was lucky to have an aunt who took me in. That was a lovely place. She was very good to me."

"Well her husband wasn't. I've been told that he used to come home drunk and beat both you and her."

"These things happen. And I was only there for three years. Until my aunt had her breakdown and I was taken into care."

"So how did that feel? Ending up in a home with no one in the world to turn to?"

"By then I was old enough to manage. The brothers there were nice enough. Some of them, anyhow."

I left it at that, made no mention of the members of the order who had been sent to jail for interfering with children in their care. I accepted that I had no right to force the wall of denial that only the man himself could decide to demolish.

"Look at this!" I overheard a mother admonish her young children. "This is beautiful." "Ooh!" chimed the children. "Isn't it beautiful?"

And on numerous other occasions: "Watch out! This is dangerous." "Help!" wailed the children. "It is dangerous, very dangerous."

So it went on, year in, year out. "This is good, that is bad. This is marvellous, that abominable." The children swallowed every word she said, without ever stopping to chew, without even looking.

She could have pointed to the black kettle and told them it was white, and they would have piped in unison: "Oh yes! Very white indeed." They were such nice, amenable children.

Watching from a distance, I sometimes felt like crying out: "For goodness' sake, don't believe everything you hear! That kettle isn't white at all, it's black! Use your eyes and see for yourselves! Rely on your own judgement!"

But of course I didn't. It wasn't my place. All I could do was hope to see the day when these children would find the wherewithal to break the bonds of their conditioning, establish a truth of their own.

They were well into their thirties before it finally happened.

I heaved a sigh of relief.

Their mother was devastated.

It is a lovely day in August, five days after my sixth birthday.

I have been sent into the garden to play. My grandmother is lying down. She has a pain in her chest.

It's unusual for her to be ill. Grandpa is the one with a weak heart.

Listlessly, I rock to and fro on the swing. I'm feeling lonely. I wish I had someone to play with.

Then, suddenly, I see just the person I need: my grandfather, on his way home from work, though it's the middle of the afternoon. "Grandpa!" I cry delightedly. "Come and push me!"

His face is white and stern, as I've never seen it before. "You shouldn't be out playing," he says gruffly, as if I was doing something I shouldn't.

"But – " I want to tell him that I'm only doing as I've been told. "It's going to rain," he adds brusquely. I look up, baffled, at the bright blue sky. Not a cloud in sight.

"Come with me!" His voice has a note of desperation.

As we walk together up the stairs, he takes my hand, holds on to it, as if he needs support. I am gripped by a sense of foreboding. But it will be some time before I realize that this moment represents the point where my childhood ends.

Growing up

From the moment our children are born, we as parents want to give them our best. Shower them with love, wrap them in security, feed and comfort them, respond to all their needs.

For how long should we be doing this? Is there ever a case for not heeding their cries? Being in a position to alleviate their distress, or, quite simply, to make them happy, why on earth shouldn't we? If nothing else, a prompt response eliminates a lot of friction.

Never mind if the children are deprived of a chance to explore their hidden resources through longing, yearning, dreaming of things they cannot have. Of the supreme satisfaction of finally obtaining something long coveted.

But imagine being the child of parents who have allowed this pattern to continue: Entering the adult world only to find that it does not cater to your every need but is full of individuals likewise deluded into thinking they come first...

Imagine seeing your relationships fail because all they are based on is want. Because you have never been taught the art of modifying your own demands for the sake of another...

Insistence on relief the minute a need arises is as bad as any addiction. Training children to survive unaided – physically, emotionally, socially – is a duty all parents owe their offspring. And the earlier it starts the better.

Would you be one of those who go through life apologizing to your parents for being what you are or, rather, for not being what they had hoped for?

If so, you are the victim of an artful, not uncommon, form of parental manipulation. Nothing is easier for a mother, or father or in extreme cases both, than instilling a sense that the offspring does not measure up to expectation.

It suits their purposes ideally: augments their ability to exert control, lessens the risk of misbehaviour and, not least, ensures continual efforts on behalf of the child to win the approval otherwise withheld.

If this hold can be maintained into adult age, the advantage grows in proportion, often transferring to the new young family, who will live in awe of in-laws and grandparents.

As they get elderly and more dependent, such parents step up their demands, making son or daughter dance attendance, terrified of doing anything to displease. Still no effort will ever be sufficient to make up for disappointing them.

Only death will break the fetters of this carefully devised entrapment. And the parents will go to their grave never having received the gift of their child's true affection.

Like most seven-year-olds, I adored my first teacher, seeing her as infinitely superior in her elevated position of authority, appointed to dispel the darkness of our ignorance.

Every word uttered by her, every scrap of knowledge she imparted, I lapped up as if it was mother's milk.

One day she introduced us to the concept of origin. "All you see around you in this class-room," she declared, "has been something else before." Now, as we pointed out different things to her, she would explain how they had started out.

A lot of pointing ensued: This desk, we learnt, had once been a tree growing in the forest... just like the copy-book... That school-bag was made from the hide of a cow... the sweater had been knitted from sheep's wool... And so on.

Thankful for an opportunity to clarify the background of an object that had long mystified me, I pointed to the bakelite electric socket.

The teacher blanched. For a moment she seemed at a loss for words. Then she composed herself and said, in a loud didactic voice: "That socket used to be... er... er... It's imported. That's it. From Africa. It grows there, on a very rare bush. Next, please."

From that moment I have never trusted authority.

"Perhaps it is the way God intended it," sighed the mother of two teenage boys, half in jest. "To make your little darlings so obnoxious that it will be a relief, not a tragedy, to see them flee the nest."

Lowering her voice confidentially, she added: "Sometimes I feel as if I can't take another day of living with so much opposition… ungraciousness… rude remarks…"

I tried to cheer her up by quoting the old Oriental wisdom that it is from those who give us most trouble that we stand to learn the most.

"Oh yes," she retorted cynically. "I've learnt my lesson. How not to bring up children. I've been far too nice to them."

The teenage conflicts that erupt in most healthy families should not be taken lightly or ignored as a passing phase. They reflect a necessary shift in family dynamics, as the established parent/child positions become outgrown.

Whether it's long harboured childhood grievances finally surfacing, or a straight-forward need for adult autonomy, teenage rebellion is a signal that an entirely new bond has to be forged.

As in all personal clashes, only mutual respect will achieve it. Keep in mind that the way you handle this passage will determine your future relationship with the adult son or daughter.

In a public ward my bed was placed opposite two teenagers hospitalized for a different reason. A precarious friendship seemed to have developed between the two.

One evening the younger one broke down and wept bitterly.

"I never wanted this," she sobbed. "It was Mum and Dad made me. And then Daniel... Daniel said he'd never speak to me again if I didn't do it."

"Come on," sneered the older girl disdainfully. "You wouldn't want a snotty brat on your hands."

Not much comforted, the grieving girl reached for her mobile phone, having made what sounded like a momentous decision: "I'm going to ring Daniel."

Her girlish voice resounded, tense and tearful, through the room: "Hi Daniel, it's me. I feel awful... No one told me it would be like this... It's as if I done something terrible... something that can never be undone. I don't know how I shall ever get over it... It's more than I can cope with... Daniel – I'm scared."

While she drew breath listening to Daniel, I think we were all wondering what his response might be. "Oh yeah?" we heard her say. "Cool. Okay, speak to you soon."

She stared into space, looking very much like the child she was. Her friend got impatient. "What did Daniel say?"

It was a moment before the girl replied: "He said he'd had a haircut."

Identity

A place where I had never expected to find myself: the ancient city of Philippopolis, capital of Thrace. A well preserved amphitheatre, golden in the morning sun.

All alone, I look around: Row upon row of concentric stone circles divided into equal sectors. Lines radiating – some reaching for infinity, others anchored by the transversal of the stage. Light and shadow playing over a balanced blend of growth, reality and potential.

Hovering somewhere near the centre of the circle, I try to work out why it all seems so familiar. Like being back in my very own landscape. Though I know that I have never been in Thrace before. Not in this life – or any other.

No – it's not the location; it's the configuration. The geometric concept that produced the amphitheatre: a Greek marriage of structure and drama, perfectly arranged.

Ever since it first entered my consciousness – whenever that may have been – this figure has persisted as my guiding star. The ideal I always reached for. Definition of my aims. It led to architecture, theatre, astrology; conditioned every word I wrote.

The essence of my mind in three dimensions, graphically depicted by the amphitheatre. It took a long time to arrive at that picture. But it was worth waiting for.

I am a transnational. One of those people who leave their country of origin, sacrifice the security of birth right, give up an established identity honed by background and education.

All for the dubious pleasure of starting anew, unconditioned, unencumbered, naked as the day you were born; even at the price of being relegated to the bottom rung of the social ladder. Everyone, down to the beggar in the street – provided he is in his own country – is better placed than a recently arrived immigrant.

Initially you struggle along, ignorant of procedures that all others take for granted, stuttering in flawed idioms, unable to assert yourself; unwittingly violating established codes and customs. You behave, and you are treated, like someone mentally and socially deficient. Courtesy and respect are in short supply.

As a clever immigrant you pick up the challenge and do your best to assimilate, fast and furiously, until your new countrymen can no longer tell that you're not 'one of them'. But is that really what you want? Go through life masquerading as something you are not, and never will be: 'one of them'?

The whole point of migrating, which by far outweighs the hardship, is the wonderful freedom it brings. The privilege of not being expected to conform. The advantage of belonging to all cultures and none. Choosing the best from each one you sample but at heart remaining your true unaffected self.

We all love people who represent an image: who take to life as if it were a stage. Acting out impressions we can easily interpret, taking their bow from the rest of us.

Some of them become cult figures: James Dean, Kennedy, Elvis, Grace, Diana – the list is long. But there are also modest examples of people pursuing symbolic lives in relative obscurity.

I'm sure you can think of a few examples of people who have successfully invented themselves: the perfect housewife ensconced in her colour-matched home; the businessman in a tailored suit taking his seat in the board-room. The bearded bohemian, the stern intellectual, the sweet-smiling bimbo, and so on. All helping us decipher the mystery of human nature by labelling themselves unequivocally.

In my younger days I worshipped such people, mistaking for self-realisation masks cultivated by their owners to the point where they lost touch with their own reality.

Perhaps that was the reason why they all died young?

I didn't see the connection. Mourning my lost idols, I did my best to follow in their footsteps. Until the day when a wise person told me:

"Dear girl, don't be tempted to live by an image. It's a much too dangerous game. To survive in this world you need substance. And an image is no more substantial than a dream."

When did you last hear someone sighing: *"Those were the days."* Was it a middle-aged woman in clothes too young for her, humming her favourite golden oldie, or a weathered man who still wears his hair long and speaks in the idiom of twenty years ago? Or – was it your own voice you heard?

You may well be one of many who are caught in a time warp maintaining an old-fashioned style; as if, at some stage, your inner watch had stopped, and everything since passed you by.

We all have traces of it, this urge to halt the passage of time; whether it is a wish for eternal youth, a nostalgic hankering for things gone by, or a vain attempt to defer the final curtain.

But then there are those who cling to an outgrown persona, because it is the only one they trust. They seem to be afraid to mature and develop; accept that each given moment offers and adds something new.

What deep insecurity lies behind such fear? Was there in their past but one occasion, when they came vibrantly alive? When they felt, finally, that they were loved and valued: someone with a right to be?

Whatever the reason, there is no escaping the fact that life is all about change and growth. You are now a somewhat different person from when you started reading this text.

'No one can bathe in the same river twice. Because everything flows.'

At six years of age, stunned by grief, I left my first home, not expecting to return.

In those days it was considered healthy to turn your back on pain. Never look back, but build a bright new future with whatever was at hand.

I grew up with a void in my heart: an ever-present sadness that I did not understand. I thought it had always been there. Part of my constitution. Until I went back.

The land between the lakes looked the same: on one side, Little Lee, frosty surface glittering in sunlight within a frame of golden reeds, streaked by long blue shadows from snow-laden trees. This was our playground in winter and summer. A haven of childhood serenity.

To the north, guarded by dark forests, shrouded by purple cloud rising as the ice settled, the vast deep waters of Large Lee stretched into the unknown. Menacing, but at the same time powerful, majestic. The steep shores – forbidden ground – were dangerously attractive.

Spanning these two was the space where my character formed, my picture of the world developed. It was my cradle – the cradle we never outgrow, although we often deny it.

Tears filled my eyes, as the wound inside me slowly began to heal. For the first time in forty years I knew the feeling of being whole.

Others

With marital breakdown and single parenthood increasing, step-families are becoming more and more common. Such relationships are never easy. Indeed, the worst mistake people make is to pretend they are.

Having witnessed first-hand the powerful emotions evoked in those involved in family arrangements not of their choosing, I can't help noting, with interest, that women who have a family and re-marry tend to be apologetic to their new partner for saddling him with another man's issue; whereas a man with a family is much more likely to be apologetic towards his progeny for replacing their mother in his affections.

In the first instance, children are made to feel that they are an undesired, undesirable appendage; in the other, the children appoint themselves critical, resentful judges of their father's choice. Neither is conducive to harmonious co-existence, or a healthy psychological climate.

We all need the family as a comfortable and secure base camp: a place to prepare for life's battles and recover in between campaigns.

All members of a troop have an equal right to its facilities. So let's forget about apologizing. Support each other, irrespective of blood ties, the way no one else will.

A man I know is a troubled soul. Mid-life, he had a breakdown. In therapy he was told to make a list of things he felt he couldn't cope with, and overleaf, write down what he most enjoyed.

"Well done," said the therapist, as he handed in his list. "That's the bulk of your work done. All that remains is for you to decide what you want to do about all these."

He started by saying good-bye to the things he didn't favour: wife, children, elderly father, drooling dog. The family home he sold at a handsome profit, which allowed him to pay off both wife and hefty mortgage.

His job was next in line: early retirement on the grounds of ill health. Then he went to live in a small apartment in Torremolinos, where he could indulge, all year round, in the two items on his list of preference: golf and windsurfing.

If he wasn't entirely happy, he was at least, at last, in therapeutic parlance, true to himself.

Two years later he was back in London receiving treatment for depression.

"This therapist is no good at all," he complained to me. "She says my problem is, I'm too selfish. If I did something to benefit other people, my health would improve dramatically. That's a complete contradiction of what I was taught before!"

"How can I do both?" he exclaimed despairingly. "Benefit others whilst remaining true to myself? It's impossible!"

As I said, he is a troubled soul.

I can recall being eaten with envy. It made me feel quite ill. The object was a girl in my school: blonde, dynamic, with glittering green eyes. Beyond being beautiful, she was wonderfully self-possessed. What else could a teenager wish for?

Her smugness irritated me no end. She was so radiant, so full of fun, so damned pleased with life. Everyone adored her, except me and a few others equally afflicted.

I nearly fainted the day she came to me requesting, would I be her friend? Seemingly sincere, she claimed to be in awe of my prowess in the classroom, where she herself had to struggle.

Resentment gave way to devotion. I became her faithful servant sunning myself in her glory; she my loyal supporter boosting my fragile self. It was a friendship made in heaven, forged for life.

Sadly, like many flares burning brightly, hers was not made to last. Shortly after her nineteenth birthday, without warning, she died.

It struck me then as absurd that, of the two of us, she should be the one who perished, while I was the one who was spared. I had always regarded her as the one who was privileged; myself as the one deprived.

I thought of my former envy and realised that, since we don't know what's in store for any of us, envy is never justified.

A friend of mine had been tyrannised by a formidable mother since the day she was born. She lived under an emotional terror-reign, where guilt was the main offensive weapon. It seemed she couldn't blink an eye without causing her mother to be hurt, upset, annoyed, distressed or worse.

"I can't take any more," she told me in despair. "My whole life is spent apologising to my mother."

"It has to stop," I agreed. "You are an adult independent woman. It's time you told her once and for all that her emotions are her own responsibility. No one has a right to blame others for what they feel."

She heeded my advice. The message, apparently, was received with ice-cold equanimity.

Some time later, my friend gave a recital – she is a very talented musician. Her mother, as usual, attended, and afterwards, with relish, pulled her daughter's performance to pieces, adding, for good measure, quotes from the audience: scathing, humiliating remarks that she purported to have overheard in the ladies' room.

Her sweet, gentle daughter burst into tears. "Mummy, don't say any more," she pleaded. "Surely you realise how much it hurts."

Her mother turned a beady eye on her: "Don't blame me, dear, for your emotions. You said it yourself: they are your responsibility."

"No," said my friend, reached by a sudden insight – perhaps the most important one she'd had. "That rule does not apply when someone hurts you intentionally."

I was every bully's dream. They were drawn to me like bees to honey. Such easy game: I must have been irresistible.

The minute someone wilfully attacked me, verbally or physically, I broke right down, burst into tears: submission, humiliation complete. Bully's mission accomplished.

How I hated myself for being so weak! For not being able to stand up for myself. It left me with a deep sense of shame.

I was too innocent to know that it isn't weakness to feel aggrieved as you discover brutality where you expected friendship, duplicity where you had placed your trust, malice where you had felt devotion.

At a later stage I learnt that this particular despair was not on behalf of my own person. I felt – still feel – that same lump in my throat whenever faced with human iniquity: tales of tortured kittens, gratuitous violence; documentaries on the Holocaust; reports of current war atrocities.

However, my lament is not for the victims, whose souls no wanton cruelty can touch; but for those misguided wretches, who deliberately have taken their leave of the only thing worth living for: the only thing that gives life value.

Rejecting and negating human kindness, they've placed themselves beyond its reach. For them there is no hope, no redemption.

Now, as my tears fall for them, I am no longer ashamed.

Duality

One of the best things in life is the offering of good company: ready laughter, easy camaraderie and, whenever needed, an ear to listen, a shoulder to cry on, a hand to hold.

True friendship, worth its weight in gold, is easy to define in that it's perfectly balanced, unaffected by privilege or position; both parties contributing to the best of their ability, and no one ever taking advantage.

The desire for friendship as an insurance against loneliness and isolation like any basic need makes us vulnerable, open to exploitation by those who use the cloak of friendship to hide a host of less honourable intentions.

Reasonably harmless are the kind who are friendly only when they stand to gain from it. Worse are those who, eaten by envy and resentment, raise themselves by lowering another; trample on one who extends a helping hand; gain control exerting insidious pressure; and delight in someone else's degradation.

Such people often masquerade as friends, but, really, they are enemies out to destroy: Extremely dangerous – and best avoided.

So watch out for the signs: beware false friends, whilst at the same time doubling your appreciation of those who prove themselves true.

I know of a young family. The woman doesn't believe in marriage. Her father was a difficult, abusive man; her mother brow-beaten, down-trodden. Determined not to risk ending up like her, she retains control of home and children.

Her partner is a good family man. He would dearly like to have legal rights to his own children, see them bear his name; be joint owner of the home they share. As it is, their mother could at any time lock the door, throw him out, walk off with a new lover, taking the children with her.

I know a couple: a middle-aged business-man and a younger, professional woman. His first marriage ended in divorce. It cost him a lot of money. Never again, he vows, will he put himself at such disadvantage.

His partner dreams of marriage and a family, but her reality is a long-term limbo. The man's friends don't quite accept her. The ex-wife won't let the children meet her. Occasions with his family place her discreetly in the background. She feels they all regard her as inferior: the one not good enough, or loved enough, to be his wife.

There must be many similar scenarios, where the ones who, for reasons of their own, won't commit themselves have it all their way; whilst those willing to give themselves freely suffer in silence.

"How is married life?" I asked a childhood friend over a cup of coffee. We were in our mid-twenties; hadn't seen each other for years. I'd heard she'd got married shortly after leaving school.

"Not all it's cracked up to be." There was no mistaking the disillusion in her voice. As she busied herself stirring her coffee, a tear fell from her eye, straight into the cup.

"He doesn't make me happy," she revealed despondently, surprising me, who had girlish illusions of marriage as a state of eternal bliss. "What about him?" I inquired. "How does he feel?"

Her reply was a blank look. I probed further: "Is he unhappy, too?" She shrugged. "Haven't you talked to him about it?" "There's no point," she said dismissively. "He's not what I had hoped for."

The girl may have been young and spoilt, but I've thought of her often in terms of relationships thwarted as a gap opens up between the expectations of one party and the failure to deliver of the other.

Who of the parties is to blame? The one making excessive, unrealistic demands, or the one who won't – or can't – measure up?

Probably both, for failing to make the necessary compromises to meet halfway.

Waiting on the quay in Roundstone, I spotted an author whom I knew slightly. With me was a friend: an intrepid woman who had spent years of her life paddling a canoe round Papua New Guinea teaching English to the native population.

We chatted with him, until the craft arrived to take us away to an off-shore island. The author stared aghast from us to the rib. "You're going off – in *that*?"

"Why ever not?" we asked, disconcerted. He shook his head incredulously. "I can't see either of you getting into a boat like that."

We leapt in like gazelles in front of him, though our morale was at an all-time low. "How did this happen?" we asked ourselves dejectedly. "How did we become so dull, middle-aged and frumpish, that other people can't imagine us having a bit of fun?"

Months later, when I next met the author, he was still going on about the two of us setting off in the rib. Annoyed, I challenged him: "What was so strange about that?"

He smiled deprecatingly. "It's just that I have a problem with boats. A kind of phobia. I wouldn't get into one of those rubber dinghies if my life depended on it."

And I noted, yet again, how easy it is to view things purely out of your own perspective, overlooking the fact that the other person is doing eactly the same.

No matter how placid and peaceful you are, it will occasionally happen that people you have no reason to dislike turn out to be your enemy. Go out of their way to spite and slander, sabotage your best efforts; injure where it hurts most.

Like any decent person, you will react to such unexplained hostility by searching deep into your memory to find the underlying cause. What could you have done to provoke such antagonism? Stepped on a tender toe? Missed an important message? You'll be anxious to put things right.

That won't be easy, however, if the crime of which you're guilty is, simply, to be yourself: something you'd be at pains to alter.

There are people who will detest you for the way you look, or talk, or smile. Nothing to do with unpleasant characteristics, wrongdoings or shortcomings. Usually it is your very best qualities that are causing the annoyance.

People of the kind who take offence where no offence is meant also tend to cultivate hatred of anyone better adjusted. They'll never forgive you and they'll see to it that you're punished.

When you next have a run-in with one of these, don't let it upset you. Just run as fast as you can, taking care to remind yourself that you're not the one with a problem.

Integration

Global warming, as the term suggests, encompasses the whole world. Environmentally unfriendly practices in the northern hemisphere accelerate the rapid melting of the ice cap in South Antarctica, which in turn has a bearing on weather patterns world-wide.

From recent research it appears that the earth's eco-systems are so closely related that reactions by Antarctic coral and phytoplankton to adapt to changing climatic conditions are echoed by similar species in northern seas, although these are not subject to the same environmental changes.

If the use of an aerosol can in some remote spot can have an osmotic impact on living organisms at opposite ends of the world, does it not follow that all things on earth are somehow intrinsically connected?

Great thinkers have long maintained that nothing exists in isolation, human beings least of all.

We are part of the same system, no less connected, no less interdependent, than the coral and plankton. Different, though, in that we retain a measure of control. We are able to decide for ourselves what we do with ourselves and our heritage.

As long as we remember just how powerful we are. Each move we make, each word spoken, each thought passing through our brain is enough to affect the world for better or, indeed, for worse.

Today's Western world sets great store by intelligence. Of all human characteristics, it seems to be the one most coveted. Everyone wants to be clever – only fools like to think themselves stupid.

The official IQ tests that have been devised to measure mental ability in figures evaluate mainly linguistic and mathematical skills. They are supposed to be independent of culture and background, but aren't these the very talents encouraged and developed in our schools?

It makes you wonder if perhaps our modern syllabus isn't far too limited. It would be nice to see things like good sense and ethical awareness promoted to serve the common good.

Not to mention emotional intelligence: the ability to handle carefully, constructively, your own emotions as well as those of others.

Imagine if everyone was taught to understand and master personal motivations and instinctive urges; trained to build harmonious relations based on insight and consideration of others... So many conflicts would be avoided, teamwork and co-operation improved, better results achieved all round.

But modern educators shy away from that which cannot be quantified. It's doubtful whether we shall ever see the study of human nature on a school syllabus.

I read in the paper about a mother, whose son had been stabbed to death for the sake of his mobile phone. She was setting up a foundation in the victim's name to help rehabilitate delinquent youths of the kind who had killed her son.

Blaming his death, not so much on the perpetrators as on the social system that had produced them: a system failing badly in its obligation towards young people in desperate need of discipline, care and control, she hoped the work of the foundation would benefit not only the individuals targeted but anyone ever to come in their way.

She finished by saying that her heart went out to those parents who had to live with the knowledge that their own flesh and blood were guilty of such an act.

In the local shop I found the article under discussion. "That mother must be a saint," uttered one elderly customer. "If that had been me, I'd have campaigned to see them hanged."

"The strength of her!" sighed a young woman. "Isn't it a wonder that she wasn't broken altogether?"

"Perhaps she came to the same conclusion as I did," said the shop-keeper, herself a widow with seven children. "That, considering the world we live in, death is not the worst thing that can happen to a person."

"One thing I can't understand," a politician once said to me, "is why one's achievements are hardly ever in proportion to the time and energy spent on a project. Ventures I give my heart and soul to come to nothing, whereas others, to which I pay only scant attention, fall neatly into place."

It reminded me of advice given many years ago by one of my teachers at drama school. "Keep going to auditions," she told the group of prospective actors. "Send out your details, pester producers. You may never get the parts you hope for, but in my experience, effort is always rewarded. An offer will come your way – though often from a direction you never anticipated."

Why is that so? I wondered then. Now I say, why ever not? How could we possibly expect to gauge in advance other people's reactions? It would be curious indeed if we could, since they have motives of their own, of which we know nothing.

But as long as we reach out, put into the world what we have of talents and commitment, like bread upon the waters it will come back – in one shape or another.

The thing to do is to keep trying, unfazed by rejection or failure, on the assumption that efforts do pay off, even though not necessarily in the way we expected.

Equality of opportunity is a fine ideal generally subscribed to. Who wouldn't agree that everyone should be given the same fair chance?

But how can we call it fair? This principle, when applied, is the very anti-thesis of equality: a cruel weeding out of those unable to take advantage of the opportunities extended.

It would be different if all contenders started at the same base line. But ask any primary school teacher to identify those seven-year-old pupils they consider unlikely to be "of much use to society". Their predictions will be largely accurate.

The little ones thus relegated to the bottom of the class will soon fall through the net and likely as not end up on the slag-heap of anti-social behaviour, crime and addiction: victims of a rigid value system that recognizes and rewards only certain narrowly defined assets.

But everyone, each and every one of us, has some potential worth exploring, something of value to contribute. There is a place and role for every person born, none more, or less, important than the other.

We all have the ability to flourish as well as the right to excel, at our own level, on our own terms.

A truly fair society is based, not on equal opportunities but on a system of equal values.

Gender

It seems to me there is no such thing as a sexually liberated woman. Liberation exists between two people or not at all.

As a concept it is by all means present in the heads of innocent young girls, who proudly look upon their bodies as assets to be enjoyed.

Unlike her mother, who regarded sex with shame and fear, through a romantic haze, today's woman is a free spirit, confident in her attractions. She walks at ease into the waiting world to sample what it has to offer on equal terms with the men.

Chances are, she may hook a fellow who can't conceive of such a thing as women's sexual liberation, but simply sees a female offering herself for free.

Depending on his level, such a man will either take advantage, break her heart, or impregnate, deceive, abandon, use, abuse, degrade, exploit her; go as far as beat or rape her.

Years later the woman will look back, wondering what destroyed her. Whatever happened to her sexuality? Her confidence? Not to mention her attractions?

It has to be said that those lucky few who team up with a like-minded partner go on to have the best of all relations, whether a fling or a lifetime commitment: an equal match of balance and respect, of shared pleasure and mutual enjoyment.

So – all aspiring liberated young women: Be very careful in your choice of mate, even for a one-night stand.

In one of our great Victorian novels I read the following pronouncement: *'The terrible curse of being poor is that we cannot afford to protect our women.'*

In the old days, rich ladies never moved without an escort, while the women of the poor were sent into the world little more than children, vulnerable, exposed, fair game to anyone.

When I grew up, my mother told me it was unseemly for young girls to go about alone at night or travel without an older companion.

I scoffed at such ridiculous conventions designed to keep demure young ladies in control. I was a child of the late twentieth century, intending to suit myself. See the world, go where I pleased, at any hour I fancied.

I can recall the thrill of freedom hitching a lift down the German motorway; solitary strolls through Paris' Latin Quarter in the early hours of the morning; illuminated baroque churches in Rome, splendid in the dead of night. Though once in London's Soho I got lost. A real thug helped me to a taxi, saying I wasn't safe there on my own.

In newspapers we read reports of women missing, raped or murdered, having mistakenly believed they were safe. The truth is, we are still as vulnerable unprotected. It's not just old-fashioned prejudice that comes in the way of our freedom. And not just fear of misbehaviour that makes our loved ones want to shelter us.

I know now that I was incredibly lucky. Some women weren't. To them, and their families, the danger became real.

Even in our enlightened days, the saying goes that women give sex for love, while men give love for sex.

It makes me think of a modern-day Casanova, who specialised in entering the homes of attractive, successful single women as they slept.

Once awake, they were subjected to a terrifying ordeal of reassurance, tenderness, affection. In the end he gently coaxed them into bed: no sign of force or violence. Indeed, he did his best to satisfy them; a few even asked him to come back.

Eventually found out, he went on trial accused of countless serial rapes. The prosecution had a hard time getting victims to testify. They were so deeply ashamed – not of having been raped, but of having offered no resistance.

The defence claimed all encounters had been consensual. His only crime was that of entering people's homes. The man himself said it was never his intention to hurt anyone. He just wished to introduce these lonesome women to the nature of true love. The only way to open up their hearts of steel was by catching them off guard. One day they'd thank him for easing off their armour of cold self-sufficiency.

The victim impact reports were decisive. His actions obviously left them with a trauma as bad as the most vicious, violent attacks.

He was given a long prison sentence. And a whole female population breathed a sigh of relief.

Women said to marry well often marry badly. I pity any bride who receives congratulations on having captured an eligible man. For this implies that she has somehow got more than she deserves; that her groom had been expected to attract something better.

Whether it is looks, age, wealth or education, background, status or any other mundane criteria, by which the world measures human value, the message comes across clearly: she is lucky; he is not.

It doesn't augur well for the woman's future. She'll be condemned to a life-long struggle trying to prove them all wrong: showing her husband's family and friends that he didn't make a mistake in choosing her.

The battle is hard to win, for no amount of hard work, self-sacrifice or moral rectitude will ever change the facts of her beginnings; gain her the esteem initially denied her.

She will always have difficulty asserting herself, even within her own family. Children detect such weakness and are quick to take advantage, which will further undermine her. Think of any spoilt, indulged or unruly children you know. Aren't they usually the product of a mother unsure of her role in the home?

It's interesting how this trap, in which so many women are caught, does not seem to swallow up men.

All one can say is: No woman should be allowed to marry, before she knows her own full worth.

On television I saw a program about zebras. Apparently, within a large herd, the males look after their families. Each one has a few females and foals, for whom he is responsible.

He leads them, drives them and directs them, shelters and protects them; seeks out water and new pastures; takes the front-line in face of any danger.

It struck me that, not so long ago, such was the role of males in our society. Men were figures of authority: instructors, guardians, providers – at home if nowhere else.

Now with women's independence, patriarchs are dying out. Instead we have two partners sharing the load. Much more satisfactory – for the women. And, I suppose, some men.

But what about all those males, shy, insecure, uncertain of their masculinity, who, unsupported by their culture, fail to make the grade? Self-assured girls pick their mates with cruel distinction: usually favouring those strong, able and aggressive.

Think of all the myriad single mothers: for each one there is a man who in days gone by would have been the head of her household. Where are all these obsolete men? What becomes of them? Are they gay? Lonely? Desperate? Part of suicide statistics?

Somewhere in the course of evolution a human strand has been lost and a pool of victims created.

Intimacy

When a man and a woman are drawn together, the attraction, I believe, is always sexual. Whether firing instantly, flaring bright, or taking its time, smouldering in secret, flickering, rekindling, before burning itself out.

The theory of love at first sight is appealing, but really, there is no such thing. Love comes later, an afterthought, once desires are sated, needs overcome, wishes fulfilled.

Sex is instinctive, possessive, commanding: a force to be reckoned with, dangerous when unleashed. Since we never know where it will take us, it needs to be handled with care.

Love, on the other hand, is never a threat. It is deliberate, fashioned by choices, generous to a fault; happy to put the other person's interests ahead of its own.

If sex is the ultimate in self-expression, love is the opposite: an on-going challenge to vanquish the self. A formidable task, much against the grain of human nature.

Our ability to love is constantly tested, as we are faced with hurdles that call for mutual negotiation. If we succeed in clearing them, the result will be a deeper attachment, greater affection, a closer bond.

Conversely, no relationship, however passionate, will survive if love is lacking. Without love we fall at the first fence.

Proponents of the 1960s sexual revolution had a noble aim in mind: to liberate us all from the age-old tyranny of insipid morality, religious condemnation, secrecy and shame, repression, guilt and inhibition.

Love was the new currency, intimacy a birthright, to be enjoyed along with carnal pleasures and made freely available as a healthy, natural means of expression.

Loneliness would be a thing of the past, every type of relationship respected; physical and emotional fulfilment available to all, with no fear of disapproval or exclusion.

Little did these humanitarians anticipate that, before long, their idealistic concept would be hi-jacked by commercial interests and used for crass material ends with no regard for any values other than financial.

Today, sex is a prime marketing tool exceeding all others. From all directions it is forced on to an unsuspecting public, sparing no one, not even little children, from the delusion that nothing but your sexuality gives you a place in the world.

How can anybody be expected to withstand this onslaught, brain-washed as we are to accept as the real thing casual couplings or mindless drunken encounters; and to live with the consequences of increased sexual violence and diseases, children who should never have been born, abuse, confusion and deviation, not to mention emotions laid waste?

Good-bye intimacy. Hello loneliness.

In the days when marriage was the only accepted arrangement for living together – or even sharing a bed – you went to the altar without asking why. (Unless, that is, a baby was on the way.)

Or else you looked to marital status for the benefits it would bring: personally, socially, materially. For anybody weak or insecure, matrimony offered a safe haven: a brand new identity supplied by the spouse.

It goes without saying that such married couples did not always live happily ever after. No one could be sure of the partner's motives. In a conflict either could say: "I married you for all the wrong reasons. Not because I loved you. Not of my own free will."

Nowadays, with no more pressure from society and little in way of incentives, you may well ask: Why should anyone want to get married?

I can't think of a single good reason… Except, possibly, a simple wish to show the world where you belong… visions of a future bleak without the other… a genuine desire to be there for the one you love, dedicating your life to his or her welfare.

For marriages entered into on these grounds auguries couldn't be better. But, my goodness, it takes courage. For any couple who have found it, I take off my hat and say: Congratulations!

As a student in London, I shared a flat with a Moslem girl.

Her mother, still young, came to visit, covered in black from head to toe: her eyes were all I ever saw of her. Proudly she told me of a solemn vow made to her husband on his deathbed twelve years before: that no man would ever see her beautiful face again.

Equally faithful is a Western woman I know, who spends her life surrounded by photographs and mementoes of a long dead husband, mourning him as fervently as once she loved him, impervious to the approaches of any other man.

Another widow with a young family remarried a man who won't hear his predecessor's name mentioned. Anything that belonged to him has been dispensed with. To the children he says: "That man is dead and gone. I'm your father now."

And then there was the Connemara workman, chatting away whilst plastering my kitchen. Having mentioned in passing that his wife had been left widowed with two little boys, he made the odd friendly reference to Jimmy, their dad.

"You knew him?" I asked. He shook his head. "We never met. But I have a feeling he's still with us, somehow, looking down from afar." Smiling, he went on: "And I say to him, don't you worry, Jimmy, I'm here. I'm looking after them for you."

I looked on, impressed, as he bent to refill his trowel.

"She fell out of love with me," sighs a man, apparently accepting this as a regrettable but perfectly valid reason for his partner in life to have abandoned him. As if 'being in love', an emotional state as volatile as any mood, were a prerequisite to staying loyal.

"He replaced me with a younger model," sniffs a middle-aged wife, fighting off bitter memories of the passion experienced early on in her marriage, before the friction and trivia of everyday life wore it all away, revealing nothing but a vacuum underneath.

The person who has no explanation to offer is one who had settled for a safe, rational union based on mental affinity and mutual interests, but came to see the other half suddenly, inconceivably, after years of congenial living, make a bid for freedom.

It seems that neither emotions, physical attraction nor common sense can be depended upon to keep a couple together. So what does it take for two people to maintain a life-long devotion? Is it love – undying love? Is there such a thing? Or is that love a function of something else?

At the end of the day, it may all come down to values. A relationship is only as sound, and as lasting, as the values shared by the two individuals involved.

Love

During a brief acting career, I appeared in an obscure play at a backstreet theatre. My part was a real challenge, furiously rehearsed for weeks.

On the second night after opening, I was aware of a strange lack of response from the house. Believing there was something lacking in my performance I tried a little harder – and harder still. No improvement.

Only in the interval was the terrible truth revealed: There was no one in the audience. I was mortified. To this day I feel the blush on my cheek when I think of myself pouring my heart out – to no one.

I quit acting soon after that. It obviously wasn't the right choice for me, if a response was so essential.

By contrast think of an artist like Renoir, who went on producing pictures, day in day out, year after year, decade following decade. Nothing ever stopped him, no amount of discouragement, poverty or failure. He painted away, regardless of people's opinions, in pure delight at his own creativity.

To be an artist merely for the return it may bring is as doomed as entering a relationship only for what you hope to get out of it: warmth, togetherness, intimacy, sex, security, money, status or whatever: The minute the reward is not forthcoming, it all comes to an end.

Love is like art: to survive it has to be genuine, sustained by its own imperative, and never requiring an applause.

A lot of people have a fear of commitment. I suppose what they really abhor is becoming dependent, handing over control. I can relate to that.

What I can't understand is why anyone should want to control another, especially in the name of love. If you attempt it, it leaves the other person with no option but to resist, evade or deceive you, or, worst of all, succumb to your will, in which case their personality expires, and you are stuck with what? A mollusc.

The symbiosis of domination, like any mutual dependence, is the enemy of love. Based on want, our greatest weakness, it makes us stunted, insecure. For if you rely on each other to fill the vacuum inside you, one of you is always bound to lose, as the other one dies, or simply moves on.

So – if you wish to find a partner: foster your independence, overcome your needs. Thus released, you'll have the best to offer: your own affluent heart.

Give freely of your love. One day you'll come across another giver, and then it will all fall into place, without any restrictions. You'll both be ready for the ultimate gift: that of commitment.

Trivia is poison for the soul. It wears you down, grates on your nerves, drives you to distraction. Mental breakdowns and stress-related illness are often due to pressures of the most meaningless kind.

As for romance, few antidotes are as effective as the trials and tribulations of normal, everyday family life. Before you know it, endless concerns of little or no significance take up your entire field of vision.

It takes something extraordinary, perhaps a brush with tragedy, to make you aware of what you stand to lose.

When a friend of ours died unexpectedly, leaving behind a wife and a young child, I wrote the following lines to my husband:

My love, when you die –
if you die before me –
I shall grieve.
Not for your passing;
I know better than that.
What can't be altered
must be borne
and gracefully accepted.
But I shall grieve –
oh how I shall grieve
for each moment of our life together
that we had and did not treasure:
precious gifts left unopened,
blossoms trampled underfoot.
Celebrations
lost forever.
Sacrificed.
Waylaid.
Oh my love, how I shall mourn them.

Many years ago in London, I was visited by a girl-friend in a highly emotional state. I was used to seeing her troubled, plagued by doomed or thwarted expectations, often lonely and depressed.

It transpired that she'd been to a seance. A male voice had sought her out, telling her, tenderly, how much he loved her, how he wished to see her happy, and how he was always watching over her.

"It was my father," she whispered tearfully. "The father I never knew. He was killed in the war, when I was a baby."

I reacted with a certain scepticism: "Do you really believe there's such a thing as spirits?"

"Who knows?" she smiled, unperturbed. "The thing is, it made me realise that he would have felt just like that. And, although he's gone, I still have his love. It is contained within me. I just wasn't aware of it before."

The woman I knew had been transformed. She stood before me radiant, secure in the knowledge that she was lovable and loved. Looking at her, I could tell that the person she had suddenly become had a rosy future ahead of her.

That moment was a turning-point for me, too. For, just like her, I had a father who died when I was a baby.

My son used to have a black-and-white pet rabbit who amazed us all. He was fully house-trained, answered to his name; he played with dinky toys and went cycling in a basket on the handle-bars.

He liked watching the early evening news, sitting on the sofa with the rest of us, occasionally operating the remote control with his hind paw, or sipping tea from my mug when I wasn't looking.

The rabbit was so much part of our life, we couldn't imagine it without him scuttling around the house.

After two years he was struck down with 'flu. The nasty kind that few rabbits survive. I rang the vet, who promised to come: a sixty mile round-trip for our precious pet.

While waiting, I took the rabbit on my lap to try and syringe some water into him. Weak, but peaceful, he lay on his side in what seemed an unnatural position. He placed his head comfortably on my arm and gave me a curious glance: not like a rabbit at all.

Later I realized it was an acknowledgement: of my presence, my care, and my love for him. For at that moment I had a rare sensation of love in its purest, most unadulterated form: love stripped of all self-interest, existing only as a mystic force.

I felt it reaching out from me, enveloping the tiny body on my lap like a protective mantle, holding him as gently as my arms, while he breathed his last.

I shall never forget the rabbit or the feeling he, like any living thing, was able to inspire.

Motherhood

In springtime, when our first lambs arrive, I go out to the sheep-pen to watch the ewes, see them nursing their young, tenderly, contentedly; licking the wet coats, bleating reassuringly.

And I say to myself, how basic the maternal instinct is. Being a mother is easy; all you have to do is follow your nature. No call for careful planning, balanced judgements, knife-edge decisions, like everywhere else in life.

Before long, however, motherhood takes on another aspect: When your treasure turns her innocent gaze upon you and says 'no'; spits out the nourishing good food you have prepared for her, stamps her little foot and announces that she hates you.

If you were a sheep, this is when you'd decide that time has come for weaning; turn your back on the offspring and enjoy chewing your grass in peace, without someone tugging at your udder.

We, of course, can't do that. Our children need us and will continue to do so, long after the maternal bond starts to give.

To love them just as much can be a challenge. But this is where we start to learn from our young: lessons of patience, empathy and forbearance.

Being a mother is no longer easy. But it does bring its own rewards.

Once I found myself in an air emergency. Before attempting to crash-land, we had to spend an hour circling to burn up excess fuel.

It was a very long hour. The stranger in the seat next to me held my hand and told me his whole life was passing before him.

My own mind was following a more morbid course, picturing my funeral, pondering whether there would be enough left of me to put in a coffin.

Then another image broke through, the agonising thought my unconscious had been fighting to suppress: the toddler I had left behind, the image of him coming into our bedroom in the morning, getting into his mother's bed to start the day with a cuddle.

I saw him entering this room day after day, with a bed that remained empty, where he would never again feel his mother's arms wrapped around his warm little body.

It was then that I realised the terrible encumbrance of parental love. How it keeps us fettered to this life, held to ransom, so that we can't even die gracefully, without our hearts being broken.

Since that day, I have only one prayer for myself: that I may live long enough to see my child able to get on without me.

My only child has just started boarding-school. The house is painfully empty. It was the boy himself who wanted to go, backed up by his father.

I resisted, with rational arguments and less rational emotions. In the end I confronted my husband and asked him why he wanted to send our son away to school. "Because I believe he would benefit," was his straight answer.

In the sleepless night that followed, I had to admit that he was right. By daybreak I had accepted that, whatever my own feelings, I had no right to hold up a process that would assist my child in his social and academic development.

And I remembered the lines my mother wrote in a notebook the day I left home to study in a foreign country:

When you were born,
I said to myself,
I shall never again be alone.
Little did I realise
that the infant I cradled in my arms
was given to me on loan,
to care for and prepare
for the day when I would hand her over,
to another life
that I can share
only from a distance.

'*Something only a mother could love.*' The phrase conjures up images of baby orang-utans, teenage hoodlums, repugnant monsters.

It does suggest that a mother's love is blind, oblivious to character disorders, to ugliness and failings; when in reality it is the other way round: maternal love is extraordinarily perceptive.

When a mother looks upon her children, she sees not only what they are, but also what they may become. In her eyes, potential supersedes limitations.

She is aware of the best in each one even when it's not apparent. Her interpretations are kind, allowing for lapses, always giving the benefit of the doubt. It says a lot about human character that, more often than not, she's proved right.

Provided she is no stranger to warm and selfless feelings, a mother will love her children for all that is contained within them, or even, at times, in spite of it; remaining constant even in the worst scenarios.

When a child has contrived to destroy anything in it worthy of affection, its mother, with deep regret, will continue to love it, partly for what it was, partly for what it might have been.

At the age of seventy, my mother was badly injured in a motor accident. I was reached by a message that she was on life support; both her legs were to be amputated.

"The poor woman," said my well-meaning neighbour. "Wouldn't it be better if she was just left to die?"

Before her last operation, she was able to talk to me. "I don't know what I'm fighting for," she said. "What sort of life do I have to look forward to, even if I do survive?"

"That's for you to decide," I answered. "Only you can tell whether life in a wheel-chair would still be worth living."

She thought for a while about this, and then she stated: "What I value most is having my children. Follow you as you grow older; see how your lives develop. Be there for you when you need me."

She survived. She recovered. Today, many years later, she lives alone, in an adapted flat, where her daily routine is much the same as usual. Except, amazingly, she's happier than before: enjoying a late blossoming.

With brand new friendships and interests to sustain her, she depends on no one; her life is her own.

But now and then she remembers that critical moment, when a mother's love for her children made all the difference.

Feelings

Ireland, 2000: The national conscience has been shattered by revelations of the ill-treatment of children in religious institutions.

Inconceivable but true: the most vulnerable members of our society, who, for a variety of reasons, did not receive their rightful share of love, care and protection, were incarcerated in homes, stripped of identity, left to starve and suffer, prey to predators who abused them.

The authorities knew about their plight but did little to relieve it. Why should anybody care about children of no consequence? They did not even have a vote!

The knowledge is disturbing but eased by the excuse that it all happened a long time ago. Thankfully, things have changed.

Nowadays, the most vulnerable members of our society, who, for a variety of reasons, do not receive their rightful share of love, care and protection, are sent out into the streets, stripped of identity, left to starve and suffer, prey to predators who abused them.

The authorities know about their plight but do little to relieve it. Why should anybody care about children of no consequence? They do not even have a vote!

It takes more than a public outcry to change the way decision-makers feel about those hapless creatures whose welfare depends on them.

A Connemara hotelier wrote a furious letter to the County Manager complaining that, in his area, renowned for outstanding natural beauty, major road repairs were consistently carried out in the height of the tourist season. If this wasn't sabotage, he growled, it was an example of extreme professional insensitivity.

The County Engineer replied, politely and regretfully, explaining that, given the Irish climate, they had no option but to repair the roads in summer, as otherwise the tar wouldn't set.

The hotel owner laughed when he told the story. "Years of anger and frustration – and all due to my own ignorance!"

I was reminded of a man I knew, whose childhood had been overshadowed by the fact that, aged eight, he had been dispatched to relatives in the country, while his mother underwent treatment for cancer. To spare the boy, nothing was said about the cause for his removal.

He suffered through many weeks, assuming that he must have done something terrible to forfeit the right to his home and to his parents' love. Even after he grew up and got his facts straight, the feeling of rejection persisted.

It's staggering to think that, even as we speak, countless lives and relationships are being ruined by virulent, destructive feelings generated by pure misconceptions.

If only everyone ensured that they were properly informed before allowing a feeling to take root, the world wouldn't be full of fools barking up the wrong tree!

The door-bell rang. A friend walked in, pale and shattered. Dark rings under red-rimmed eyes, lips quivering from restrained emotion. "She's left me," he whispered, as if expecting the words to hurt. "After fourteen years of an ideal marriage, she's upped and left me."

I couldn't help thinking of his wife telling me in confidence that the marriage, to her, was a prison: a locked cell, stifling and restrictive; no access to daylight or fresh air. "I shall have to break out," she had stated calmly, "or else go under."

"I love her," he said brokenly. "Since the day we met, I've only lived for her. My life was dedicated to her welfare. Without her, I have nothing."

It crossed my mind that this degree of spousal devotion seems to come more naturally to men. I wonder if it stems from an unconscious yearning back to the blessed state of infancy, when all their requirements were filled by a bountiful madonna who asked for nothing but submission in return.

"Could it be," I ventured carefully, in an attempt to help, if not comfort, "that your relationship has been based on your needs more than hers?"

"Not at all," he snapped, offended. "I never had a thought for myself. I gave her everything, each living moment. Body and soul, I was all hers." Bewilderment took over, as he pondered: "How can any woman walk away from such devotion?"

I didn't have the heart to tell him. Perhaps one day I will.

Of all emotions, the most dangerous are those we don't know we have. They are the cause of rash, impulsive acts; they drive us to be erratic, distort our sense of judgement.

It's natural enough to want to close the door on feelings that are painful or unworthy. But suppression has an awful lot to answer for in terms of devastation.

Does that mean the other extreme is more healthy? Emotions erupting at short notice, making us scream and shout, laugh or cry, with little or no restraint?

One thing is certain: the more easily a feeling manifests itself, the more superficial it is. Falling back on moods to let off steam, indulge ourselves, or even manipulate others, is a means to an end not altogether honourable.

Emotional responses need not affect our conduct. Like spoilt children, they crave attention, but once we recognize them, they settle down, leaving us free to accept them as being there, somewhere in the background, though no more important to our life than the twinge you register when a needle pricks your finger.

The purest, most sacred feelings are those we encounter deep inside ourselves in moments of solitude and peace. Such feelings crave no tribute, answer to no needs. They are, in themselves, what we consist of.

Forgiving an enemy is but a sweet pleasure. After all, it is entirely in your own interest to rise high above your adversary in integrity and dignity. Nothing crushes a person of ill will like the opponent's magnanimity.

It's different when a loved one inflicts a wound, lets you down, tramples all over your heart. How could you forgive them? That would lessen the impact of the damage done, play down the transgression; almost, you might say, condone it –

when what you really want is to compound their guilt, draw attention to the crime for which no remorse is sufficient. Punish them for your pain, even at the expense of destroying your own self.

Bitterness is a disease; the only cure forgiveness. But not everyone is capable of summoning the inner strength required for such a feat.

Therefore, it is advisable to forestall situations that call for these heroic deeds, by acknowledging hurt openly and honestly, at an early stage: before the wound begins to fester.

Another safety device is for your own part to ensure that nothing you say or do could become a hot bed for such dangerous deep resentment.

It is the need for forgiveness, as much as the lack of it, that kills relationships.

Life

Do you have a main objective? An overriding ambition that you intend to get around to one day? Once the children are grown up, the mortgage paid, the garden planted? When you get a better job, retire, win the Lotto?

We potter away, consumed by all those little tasks that keep us from attending to things that really matter. Waiting, waiting for the day when we will finally come into our own.

Frustrated, unfulfilled, we trundle on, completing one lap after another on our everyday obstacle course, while our dreams evaporate on the horizon and the goalposts keep shifting.

Then, suddenly, an exit appears! A wide-open path to self-realisation. Likely as not, we turn the other way: focus on yet another obstacle.

Is the effort too much? The shocking impact of sudden change? Or is it a pathetic fear of failure that makes us cling to limitations whenever freedom is within reach?

But fulfilment needn't be a trauma. As long as you set your sights within your capabilities, and then make it a matter of priority, allowing nothing in the way of your endeavour.

With your eyes fixed upon the target you can add a tiny brick each day. Work away, unnoticed, unperturbed, until, sooner or later, you see it emerge:

That impressive structure: your lifetime achievement.

Like many others, I am hooked on the dreaded Sudoku. No day is complete without the solution of at least one of these wordless puzzles.

What is it about the Sudoku that makes it so addictive? Eighty-one squares, like so many days ahead (or years, hours or minutes), some offering clues to the perfect formula, others empty, waiting to be filled, methodically, meticulously, with your choice of numbers, each the unequivocal outcome of the one that went before.

As with all exercises in logic, you know when you've got it right. But God help you if you mess up. One lapse – and the whole thing collapses. Then you have to retrace your steps, find the error of your ways, make suitable amends, often with considerable effort. It must be done – to avoid the dismal failure of having to abandon a stranded Sudoku.

You soon learn that with a cool head, a clear focus and steady concentration, such disasters need not happen. Even with the diabolical variety: complex labyrinths of thought, rife with false trails and red herrings, instinct usually brings you home.

The Sudoku: ideally pure and simple, a beautifully balanced weave, where all is interconnected, transparent, self-confirming; nothing left to chance.

Why can't life be like that? But then, who says it couldn't?

"Is there such a thing as fate?" asked a young man at a party. A welcome change from the usual inconsequential chit-chat.

I told him I did not think so – but I did believe in destiny. He looked at me perplexed. "That's the same thing!"

I took a deep breath, but before I could begin, he had been spirited away by a siren with long blonde hair and purple finger-nails. So I never got a chance to tell him that fate, in my view, is pre-determined, whereas destiny we hold in our hands. It's a deliberate fulfilment: the management of personal resources, potential moulded by our own free will. It is determined by the moves we make, at each juncture, each given moment.

Events may hit entirely unforeseen, impossible to check, prevent or further. But the response is up to you. You decide how it is going to affect you: externally, internally, for better, for worse.

See your changing circumstances as markers on your way. Read them and choose which ones to follow: that way you remain in charge.

All this I wanted to say to the nice young man at the party. Now he'll have to find his own answers, which is perhaps as well.

At least he's made a good start asking that vital question.

As a young adult, having just received a rewarding but not very marketable arts degree, I found myself staring vacantly into the abyss of my future. So many possibilities, so many perils! Endless potential, for success as well as failure; irrevocable choices waiting to be made. I was caught between fear and desire: a paralysing dilemma.

Then I was given this advice by an old family friend, who himself had excelled in life:

"Base no major decisions on your own needs and ambitions: that's like looking at the world through the wrong end of a telescope. To succeed you must forget what you want; instead, develop and offer what you've been given."

So this was it, the rite of passage into the great big world: to look beyond your own person, accept yourself as a component consigned to playing your part in a large universal structure.

In due course I discovered he was right. By contributing what I had, to the best of my ability, I found the strength and confidence I needed to go forward. And if I didn't achieve all that I had hoped for, the effort brought as much satisfaction as the result.

Away from personal gratification, choices are easy. There are no anxieties, no regrets; no humiliation, no disappointment. What you gain is the inner peace of knowing that, whatever happens, you did, and gave, your best.

You ask me why I do it. Why work so hard? All this pain and exertion for such fickle returns?

How can I explain to you that I don't have a choice in the matter? My work is my conscience, a whip and a spur. It drives me out of bed in the morning, sends me on errands in dark places, where no one can follow.

What am I searching for? The spring of *aqua vitae?* Fuel to feed my fire? The answer is: anything to keep me going. Keep me alive.

When, occasionally, I run out of steam, I think of my friends out there: anyone who would, could, might one day read and relish what I write. Unknown thousands – or just one; they are my reason and my excuse to continue.

It gets lonely at times here in this capsule of self-imposed labour, the nature of which no one seems to understand, not even those who know me well. It would take someone like you, who are close enough to see it from my end.

Don't look upon my work as a rival taking me away from you, but as my way of life, the only one. A worthy objective, which, if shared, will only bring us closer together.

Religion

On principle, I hold with the view that everyone has a religion. If you define the word as an inner conviction, it will include even the atheist, and the agnostic.

Psychology suggests that our relationship with God is conditioned by our links with authority in general. Perhaps the truest manifestation of a culture can be detected in its religious attitudes.

Having said that, I recall being in a shop in Sweden, ordering something, quoting my home address. "Ireland?" said the shop-assistant, a spry lady in her sixties. "What is it like? Any different from here?"

Choosing from a myriad examples, I told her briefly that Irish families tend to be larger. Children could number ten or eleven, even fifteen, sixteen.

"Sixteen children!" cried the grey-haired lady, a look of horror on her face. Then she leant confidentially over the counter and uttered in a hushed voice: "Is this because Irish men are particularly... *insistent*?"

Smiling, I explained that the Catholic Church does not approve of family planning: "It is considered wrong to take such precautions if it is God's will that a child be conceived."

"God's will!" she exclaimed. "But he doesn't exist!" And then, seeing my baffled face, she went on: "I mean, that's common knowledge – *nowadays*."

I left the shop, reflecting that here was one person who was truly void of religion.

My first religious crisis came at the age of eight. Up until then my relationship with God had been problem-free. I liked the idea of a kind father in Heaven guiding my step, prompting me to be good, sending his guardian angel to protect me against anything nasty or dangerous.

But then I received religious instruction at school. The teacher was a puritan: you could tell from her forbidding black dress and the way her thin grey hair was pulled back in a tight bun. The only thing alive on her was a pair of nut-brown eyes burning with religious fervour, and never more so than in divulging the story of Man's Shameful Fall.

"God knew how to deal with disobedience," she announced triumphantly. "He said to Adam, you'll pay dearly for this. You will carry the burden of your guilt for ever; no generation will be spared. Get thee out of Paradise, to earn thy bread in the sweat of thy face, till the day when it pleases me to turn you to dust!"

Poor Eve fared no better. She was told she would bear her children in sorrow and anguish; her desire would be her wretched husband's: he would rule over her.

I listened in dismay, as this new face of God emerged: mean and vindictive, petty and cruel. Light-years away from the merciful father I had got to know and love.

You can't trust anyone, I concluded despondently. To fly off the handle like that – and all for the sake of an apple!

There are those who turn to our Lord only in times of need; look upon Him as a kind of insurance policy activated by their humility.

One could say that their supplications are normally heeded – as long as they accept that no is also an answer; that delay does not constitute denial; and that the granting of a request frequently carries a price tag.

It's not unusual for people to get exactly what they prayed for and then spend the rest of their days wishing they hadn't.

Like friends of mine who were in dire financial straits, having overextended themselves building the house of their dreams. With all avenues of credit exhausted, they found themselves with three days to produce ten thousand pounds – or else lose their home.

In desperation, for the first time in decades, the wife went down on her knees and pleaded with the God she hardly knew to send them the required amount.

The next day her husband came home from work and – miraculously – handed her a cheque for ten thousand pounds. It was a redundancy payment. His job, their sole source of income, had been lost.

Lacking the perspective that only hindsight will provide, we are not ever in a position to determine what's in our own best interest. Therefore, we might as well leave it to Providence to mete out what we deserve, whilst we pray for the strength of mind to recognize and honour our rewards.

"How do you like your new neighbour?" I asked an elderly Swedish relation in an old people's home. "He's a nice enough man," was the reply. But then he added disapprovingly: "Though he's *religious*. Keeps going off to church."

At home in Ireland, I had heard one neighbour speak respectfully of another: "A splendid woman. Deeply religious. Goes to Mass every day."

Two opposite views, you may think. Yet both expressed the same popular misconception: that all who go to church are religious and, implicitly, that all who are religious go to church.

But people may go to church for a variety of reasons: social, cultural, habitual. Some may be seeking a place to belong, or a chance to hand over the burden of moral decisions.

Religion, then, is something quite different. Deeply personal, hidden from view, defined by faith and conscience, it is reflected mainly in your attitude to life: what you find in it of value, how you choose to commune with the world.

If you are lucky enough to find that the rituals of your particular church coincide with your idea of religion, you will have access to a rich fund of spiritual support and guidance. It doesn't mean that you are more pious than all those who go it alone. Only that you are less isolated.

The cathedral of Saint-Sernin, Toulouse: a Romanesque master-piece, built by a faith that moved mountains, literally, stone by stone. Turning them to arches soaring heavenward, higher and higher, like souls yearning for release, in bluff defiance of existing building techniques.

Seen piecemeal, arch upon arch, what you perceive is substance; diverse elements ranged sequentially. Yet the dynamics wrought by light and obscurity, space and matter, optical illusions, transform the structure into one single chord: a keynote deep and sonorous.

Like so many of our disjointed life experiences: bereft of meaning until you step away and allow the full picture to emerge. The picture that, once seen, is never doubted.

Who said there is no life in stones? This goes beyond bricks and mortar. The twelve identical stone vaults in their ever-diminishing perspective draw you gently but irrevocably towards the cathedral's heart: the site of the high altar reposing within an ambulatory brimming with brilliant light.

Grace within reach. Comfort beckoning. A vision of ultimate peace. Nine hundred years old and just as real today.

Faith is fed by many sources. For me Saint-Sernin is one.

Mind

Have you ever found that, in sharing a memory, especially with someone you know well, your recollections differ? Even within a closed circle, the records of the past emerge with astounding discrepancy.

Like the occasion of Mary's wedding: "What a terrible, stormy day. – "Not at all, the sun was shining!" – "It was calm, but pouring with rain."

"And when Billy came back from Germany in his beautiful brand new car..." – "What do you mean, it was an old banger!" – "I'm quite sure he came on the bus."

One person recalls minute details, where other minds are blank. There seem to be as many versions of a story as there are people telling it.

How can we expect our impressions of the past to be historically accurate? We all have our own method of selecting, sorting and storing files for our personal archives. That material is uniquely ours: we are what we remember.

But if memories are merely individual takes on reality, does it not follow that somewhere, in amongst them, hides a deeper truth? And if we're brave enough to go beyond them, follow the trail they lay, it will lead us to the source and, finally, reveal all: not just what actually happened but also how it affected us.

Here is a little mind-game to play with yourself and others:

Close your eyes. Imagine yourself walking along a road. Describe in detail what it's like: rough or smooth, wide or narrow, going uphill or downhill? Surrounded by a verdant landscape or hemmed in by sombre man-made edifices? Bathed in sunshine or drenched by rain? What time of day is it?

Now you come across a fence. What does it look like? High, low, flimsy, solid – to the left or the right? Or blocking your path, calling for negotiation? Next you look out over some kind of water: Would it be a wide ocean? A crystal-clear, fast-flowing river? Perhaps a murky stagnant pond?

Suddenly you find a key: Is it old and rusty, or new and shiny? Would it be of any use to you? Do you pick it up?

Finally, you arrive at a building. What kind? A modern block of flats? A quaint old cottage? Do you enter it? What happens next?

The exercise is supposed to be a blue-print of your present life situation, as experienced by yourself. The road, of course, is your walk through life, the fence any obstacle you're facing, the water your stimulus, the key possible solutions, the building your point of security, etcetera.

Viewed in that light, did it reveal anything that you didn't know before? If so, it is your unconscious speaking, symbolically, the way it does in dreams.

On a few rare occasions I've had the odd sensation of remembering things that haven't yet happened.

Impressions come to me, seemingly insignificant, like a dream recalled: some parts well-defined, others nebulous. A distinct ambiance instantly recognisable once the event occurs.

The window of an antique shop, a light rain falling, myself in a black mackintosh: That moment came about one day much later in Pimlico Road, London.

A magnificent pink camellia in a sun-dappled conservatory: I waited half a lifetime to see that realised.

And for years I was haunted by an unidentified sound emanating from our hall, associated with a vague form, half-endearing, half-annoying, existing somewhere level with my knees.

The mystery was solved eventually by my three-year-old pedalling his trike with an array of noisy toys attached to the back of it. Round and round on the flagstones of the hall, relishing the clatter it created.

These experiences make me wonder if time exists at all. Perhaps it's just a concept invented by ourselves to bring order into chaos; to enable us to learn lessons from the past?

Or, else, time does exist, but it stands still, while we are the ones who keep moving. But in that case, what's the point of occasionally going too fast?

It is a well-known fact that authors are unable to proof-read their own work. Even the most pedantic professionals fail to notice typographical errors and omissions. It's as if, knowing what the text contains, they see only what's supposed to be on the page: words and lines as they were intended, not as they actually appear.

Similarly, in our daily life, we tend to acknowledge only that which is familiar, expected, welcome, validated. Mistrusting anything that belies the shackles of our private conventions, we embrace reality as we understand it, not necessarily as it is.

The mind can't be relied on to be objective, subject as it is to influences of all kind, many of which we're not even aware of. Reason, though never doubting its own integrity, can be easily prejudiced, swayed and corrupted.

To find the real truth – the truth that nothing can distort or challenge – you have to disregard the evidence before you, forget those rational deliberations and instead, take guidance from within: rely on inklings... instinct... intuition.

Your inner vision will tell you more than the intellect ever could.

"Humble? Me? You must be mad!" exclaimed my friend, unwittingly confirming the allegation. He was a man of grandiose gestures, a host of sumptuous parties featured in gossip columns. But then, why should humility be the exclusive domain of the dull and mousy?

At heart he was quite shy, the way all sincere people become self-conscious under scrutiny, because they have nothing to hide behind: no affectations, no false veneer.

He confided to me he was in serious financial trouble. Myself young and poor, I dismissed it: "Never mind. As long as you have your health." He smiled. "I'd rather be a rich invalid than a healthy pauper." – "You'll be all right," I told him. "Anyone with your talent for friendship has little to worry about." He was a wonderful friend to many, many people.

A shadow passed over his face. "What's the point of having friends if you have nothing to offer them?"

That's when I accused him, with a laugh, of selling himself short. I was too inexperienced to know that such excessive humility is a serious distress signal.

Anyone who believes that his own person stripped of assets would be of no value to others, also suffers from the delusion that his actions lack the power to hurt or damage anyone. It is a most dangerous mindset and it should never be passed over.

My friend died of an overdose three days after going bankrupt.

Freedom

'I'm alone in a house by the sea,
with nobody else for company.
Alone with my sorrow,
my hopes, and my dreams.
Alone in a house by the sea.'

These lines I wrote many years ago, in response to my first ever taste of complete solitude.

The remote homestead, the spectacular landscape and, above all, the peace, unbroken from morning till night, the silence, undisturbed for days even by the grating sound of my own voice, brought an intensity to my experience of life that I have treasured ever since.

Many people abhor loneliness, dread it as an enemy, fear its knock on the door. I wish I could convince them that solitude and silence, its faithful companion, are the best friends anyone can have.

They ask for nothing in return, have no expectations, exert no pressure, never let you down, never interfere, are always there for you; allow you like no other to exist simply as yourself, in a state from which you will always re-emerge stronger.

What's more, no matter how stressful your surroundings, you can always escape to it, time and again, as often as you like; revisit this exquisite state, if only in your head.

At a school get-together, parents got on to the subject of confirmation. One mother voiced the often-heard opinion that it shouldn't all be a question of presents and new clothes; if the youngsters didn't understand the ritual, they shouldn't be confirmed at all.

"Why make an issue of it?" one laid-back man said equably. "If my daughter wants to go along with her friends, that's fine with me. If she doesn't, that's okay, too."

"Well we certainly won't let our children go through with it," another father asserted. "We intend to impose nothing on them in terms of faith."

"But that's a paradox," a timid-looking woman ventured. The man turned towards her and stated with authority: "Religious freedom is a basic human right."

"Which you are denying your children," the woman went on, undaunted. "They will be free to choose what they like," the father insisted, annoyed. "But you leave them no option. If you give them nothing, nothing is all they'll ever have."

Somewhat less confident, the man muttered: "So what do you suggest?"– "I would offer them something to believe in, together with the right to reject it."

The father reflected for a moment, then smiled defeatedly. "Okay. I see what you're getting at. I'll give it some thought."

Little more was said after that. It seemed they had all got something to think about.

"How did you manage it?" asked a young friend, who had been suffering from depression. "What did you do to become so independent, happy and fulfilled?"

I had to stop and think. Years of anything but happiness flashed by: loneliness, anxiety, terror. It took me some days to find the answer.

When I did, I rang him up and said: "I got rid of my baggage. Put it down and walked away. Not an easy thing to do, but I had discovered that the stuff I was lugging around wasn't really mine, it was debris left over from other people's travels. They had piled it on to me, but I had no use for it.

"For a while I felt naked – vulnerable, exposed. Much of my identity had been stuffed into those bags. Briefly I feared that I would not be able to survive without them. "But then – for want of other options – I took a deep breath and listened.

"And from the hidden depths of my own being came another note, another truth: A conviction never to be challenged. A sense of belonging extending beyond all limits, needing no affirmation other than the fact of my own existence."

A beautiful birch on our land had toppled over in a storm.

It was a pathetic sight: this tree that had stood, tall and majestic, spreading its magnificent crown of rich green foliage, suddenly reduced to a piece of debris.

The reason was plain to see: its roots, torn from the earth and exposed to the light of day, had been far too shallow to support the extravagant growth above ground.

It made me think about roots: the tendency of some to cling to theirs to the point of suffocation, rather than engage in the perilous task of cutting their own furrow; while others triumphantly flee the nest, up, out and away, never to look back, going as far as to deny their origins for a chance to live life entirely on their own terms; and then, how both these extremes restrict personal freedom. To avoid being stunted, we must grow above our roots, but at the same time we need them in order to realize our full potential.

For if we expand too far, without first tending to the part that connects us to the earth, making sure it's stable and secure and deep enough to provide an anchorage, we risk ending up like the beautiful birch: felled to the ground by a storm.

An adoptee from far away, I've spent nearly half my life living in Connemara.

The place I was born to was quite different: a park-like landscape, dappled by the sun, pretty and sheltered, neatly tended through centuries of prosperity. Trees sighing softly in a summer breeze; tidy gravel paths for lakeside walks, water lapping gently at your feet.

Those impressions dwindled to a wistful memory, when I found myself exposed to the harsh conditions of this extreme western edge of Europe. A bleak wilderness of vast open spaces bordered by a jagged mountain range. Stony reaches pelted by heavy downpours, ravaged by storms devastating the little growth they yielded.

Today, the evidence of age-old poverty and starvation has mercifully been eclipsed by the advance of the Celtic tiger.

And as my eye wanders unrestricted over bogs and meadows that know no boundaries, no limits... across the wide Atlantic Ocean swelling with the tide in an echo of my own pulse, reaching for horizons ever shifting, ever new... I am in no doubt that here is my home. My bedrock of complete security and total freedom.

Where the heart is at peace there is no need for shelter.

Suffering

When you look back on your past, how many black holes do you detect? Periods of your life too dark, too painful, or perhaps too shameful, to remember?

We all have them. It's a natural instinct to try to protect our equilibrium by ignoring memories that hurt. What could possibly be gained from dwelling on past distress? Surely it's healthier to look forward, with faith, and hope, and optimism, to better things ahead?

But the pain buried deep inside does not go away. It festers, like a foul abscess, spreading its poison, causing no less damage because you choose to neglect it. Wounds need light and air to heal. They'll never do so unless they are brought to the surface.

What's more important: each significant life experience, no matter how traumatic, contains something of value: if nothing else, a measure of added depth and insight. To bury that, along with the other stuff, means depriving yourself of vital personal components that you can't afford to be without.

I've learnt from my own experience. Until quite recently, my past was full of black holes. Exploring them I know can be daunting, difficult and not without danger.

But by God, it's rewarding.

"Help!" squeaked a mouse to the cow. "The farmer's set a trap for me! I'm terrified of getting caught." The cow chewed its cud. "So? What's that to do with me?"

Next he opened his heart to the pig. "Don't come bothering me," said the pig, wallowing in the mud, "with things that don't concern me." The hen was slightly more sympathetic. "I know exactly how you feel, my dear, but honestly, it's your problem."

In the night, a deadly snake got itself caught in the mouse-trap. And when the farmer's wife tried to release it, she was bitten. Before long she was gravely ill.

Devastated, the farmer sacrificed his only hen to cook her favourite dish: anything to make her better. But she was too ill to eat.

All her family moved in to help nurse her back to health. Food was scarce but they had to be fed. The farmer had no option but to kill the pig.

In the end, despite their efforts, the farmer's wife passed away. There was a big funeral. The cow had to be slaughtered. And so, in the end, only the mouse survived.

This story may be worth remembering the next time you are tempted to dismiss a distress call from another person as being none of your business.

Every now and then I have reason to recall a woman I know who fell head over heels in love with a wonderful man. He was kind, affectionate, good-humoured, charming and very attractive; intelligent, hard-working, successful. No drawbacks or secret vices. In short, ideal husband material.

Luckily, feelings were mutual. It wasn't long before they were engaged to be married. Both families rejoiced, everyone got on famously.

I was delighted for my friend, whose life had not always been easy. She deserved all the happiness she could get.

Then, not far off the date set for the wedding, she shocked her fiancé, as well as her family and his, by breaking off the engagement.

"Why?" I asked her incredulously. "I've never known a man who had so much to offer a woman."

She nodded in agreement. "I know. But by and by I realized that I couldn't share my life with him. Something was missing. One dimension, which to me is essential."

I sat in silence for a while, trying to figure out what this might have been. She looked at me, almost apologetically, and said: "He had never known suffering."

I think I know what she meant.

A friend told me after losing her daughter: "The grief is hard enough to bear. But then, added to it, is the shift in one's own identity. From being a mother like any other, I've become the woman whose child died. It takes a lot of adjusting."

Her words brought back memories of my early days: how I had dreamt of being a perfectly ordinary young girl: living an ordinary life, in an ordinary family, to whom, by definition, extraordinary things did not happen.

I wanted to be like the other children I knew: happy, carefree, confident, secure. Not stigmatised, exposed, vulnerable.

Never acknowledging the tragedies in my past, I guarded them like a guilty secret, more ashamed of being sad and unfortunate than of being false and insincere.

But no matter how hard I tried to cover up, no one was ever fooled. The afflictions had left their marks: I carried them around, as clearly as a placard on my chest.

I wish someone had told me then that each trauma, each bereavement, each moment of suffering we live through, far from lessening our value as human beings add to it, like jewels in a crown.

And even if the weight on your head is heavy – wear that crown with pride. It's a token of your humanity. A badge of honour.

At a fun fair, on a lovely summer's day, waiting with my son to board a giant roller coaster, I noticed ahead of us in the queue a couple with a boy of about nine. He was very quiet, painfully thin, white as a sheet; his bald head suggested chemotherapy treatment.

The parents did their best to humour him: concerned, solicitous, noticeably anxious that he should have a good time. Laughing, joking, the father tempted him with a wad of pink candy floss. The boy just shook his head dejectedly.

Then, amongst all the happy, excited children, he began to weep, silently, profusely. The mother picked him up, off the ground. He was really too old to be carried, though light enough.

She went to sit on a bench nearby, cradling him as if he were a baby. The child curled up on her lap, sobbing helplessly into her shoulder. Over his head the parents' eyes met in a look of helpless despair.

I looked away, regretting my intrusion on such a private occasion. The grief, for which all three of them knew there was no consolation, and in which, but for the grace of God, I had no part.

Yet these strangers left me something of value that I hope to retain till the end of my days: A reminder of the gift of life, and health, so precious, so precarious. A reason to cherish each moment we have with our loved ones; to take not a single day for granted.

Courage

Have you ever been exposed to a situation, where your capacity for courage was stretched to the utmost? Or did you perhaps see someone close to you being put to a test of bravery beyond anything they'd been prepared for?

If so, you may have come to discover that courage is a finite human resource. Whatever your individual threshold of endurance, if you keep drawing from this source with nothing to replenish the supply, it will eventually dry up.

Throughout history, wars have been determined by a sudden collapse of morale amongst the troops. Any able military commander knows that the vital commodity of courage cannot be taken for granted. In demanding circumstances it has to be watched, nurtured and boosted, like a leaking vessel that needs constantly topping up.

Anyone who has had the startling experience of courage failing at a time when it's badly needed will know the value of comfort and support from others. When life's challenges become overwhelming, a word of compassion, a hand to hold, may be just what we need to revive our flagging spirits.

Therefore, whenever we see a friend or a loved one struggling to be brave, we should never hold back but do all we can to put into practice the meaning of the word "encourage".

I'm sure you've come across little children who take fright at the silliest things: insects, clowns, remote control cars. Anything they don't recognize or fathom send them screaming to their mothers, whose instinctive reaction is to comfort them with hugs and kisses.

Not realizing that this response may condition their treasures, even as adults, to indulge irrational fears, in the unconscious expectation of tender rewards – only to end up cruelly disappointed.

Would it not be better to welcome each needless manifestation of fear as an opportunity to boost the child's morale by prompting it to examine the object of its terror: establish beyond doubt that this is something not worth being afraid of?

Fear overcome will vanish rather than rankle, leaving only the imprint of its defeat, together with the confidence and security derived from the knowledge that you are able to confront and defuse the things that scare you.

So, if you ever see your children terrified, don't pet and pamper them, but give them a chance to build up the courage they'll need for a life of richness and fulfillment.

Only exposure to an element of danger will help them develop their best possible protection, whatever is in store:

A character that will always triumph over events.

I was talking to a woman, whose teenage son had disclosed to his parents that, as a child, he had been sexually abused by a neighbour.

Knowing that it wouldn't be a pleasant experience, they agreed together to report the man. The boy felt the main thing was to protect other children from having to suffer the same.

For the same reason, when it came to trial, he waived his right to anonymity, so that the man could be exposed and other victims urged to come forward.

Throughout, the parents did all they could to support him. They kept commending his courage, told him to keep his head high. He had nothing to be ashamed of. He had done no wrong.

A few years later, the boy became seriously involved with a girl who knew nothing of the case. He realized he would have to tell her – before someone else did.

"And that," said the mother to me, "was when I realized that his bravery had not been without a terrible price to pay."

When she asked him what the girl's reaction had been, he replied: "It's all right, Mum. She still wants to go out with me."

"I think you must be the bravest person I have ever come across," said one fellow attending a talk given by my mother on the subject of rehabilitation.

Aged eight-four, confined to a wheel-chair, she didn't share his view.

"This woman is putting us all to shame," muttered another man. "Here I've been miserable for a whole week because of an ingrown toe-nail…"

"Well that at least," smiled my mother, a double amputee, "is a problem I don't have to contend with."

She continued on a more serious note: "I don't need a pair of legs to enjoy life. As long as I can wake up to a perfectly ordinary day, see the sun shining, hear the birds sing… have my friends and loved ones… little in the way of worries, no more pain than I can bear…"

"But surely," someone else interjected, "there must be days when you wished the accident had never happened?"

"What good would that do? Distress myself with imaginings of life as it isn't, never will be? Dwell on futile comparisons to those whose circumstances are different – not necessarily better, for all I know.

"Preferable by far is to embrace life within the limits of your own reality. Accept the here and now, on whatever terms you've been given. And that," she concluded, "applies not only to people in wheel-chairs."

The taxi driver apologized for having kept me waiting so long. "We were told the airport was closed. On account of the emergency."

"I was in it," I sighed. He stared at me. "Oh my God! You were one of those!"

As he passed a long line of fire-engines on their way back to base, the driver told me he'd been having breakfast with his three little girls, when they heard on the radio that an aircraft with sixty-three passengers on board was in serious difficulty in the sky above Dublin.

"It brought tears to their eyes," he said. "They got down on their knees and started to pray for you all."

I told him then about the strange experience I'd had mid-air. How all of a sudden, as I faced what could well have been my last ten minutes of living, my fear had gone away. I felt calm, not to say serene. "Perhaps it was something to do with your daughters' intervention. I'd like to think it was."

"Well now," he replied modestly. "They wouldn't have been the only ones."

I said to him: "Please tell your girls that I was helped by their prayers. Let them know that a kind thought has the power to give strength and courage to another."

In the rearview mirror I could see him smile. "I'll tell them that all right. What's more – I'll make sure they never forget it."

Soul

In my teens I befriended a neighbour's son called Benny. Benny was like any normal twelve-year-old. The only problem was, his body was over thirty. But he was happy and good-natured; I enjoyed his company.

His mother said, he had done well at school. They all had high hopes for him. I waited to hear more, and eventually, with infinite sadness, she told me about the accident.

Apparently, Benny had had an older brother whom he idolised. A kind, protective young man who played the guitar and rode a motor-bike. One day, entreated by his little brother, he took him for a spin.

That was the evening when some mindless vandals had decided to torture a horse, wrapping its head in loops of barbed wire. The wretched animal, driven to insanity, bolted on to the main road, right in the path of the motor-bike. Brother and horse were killed on impact. Benny escaped unhurt. But he was never the same again.

His mother wiped away a tear. 'It is as if some part of him, the most vital part, cannot bear to go beyond that event.'

I wish we could all do the same: preserve our innocence, remain in that sacred space we inhabited up until the moment of our first confrontation with evil.

How do you help a person heading off down the wrong avenue? The following I wrote to someone close, whose selfish, destructive manner, and obsession with her own physical comfort, had left me deeply concerned.

My dear – where is your soul?
I know it exists,
I remember it from days gone by.
My dear – hold on to your soul!
You cannot afford to lose it.

It's easy enough to live by your body's dictates,
succumb to its wishes, follow its every whim.
But sooner or later, the flesh lets your down.
And where will that leave you?

Don't fall for the cruel belief
that the body is all you've got,
but see it as the humble servant of your self:
an obedient tool helping you realise
your highest ambitions.

Forget your matter and seek your soul,
find it, nurture it,
with all means at your disposal.
It is your only protection
against the body's relentless decay
that sets in the moment you're born.

You who are no longer young,
be aware that your soul will lift you
above disease and suffering,
pain and degradation,
safeguarding your dignity
until the day you die.

I'm saying this as someone who was there,
who reached the end,
touched the stars,
and glimpsed eternity.

By way of reply she suggested that I seek professional treatment.

When I look back upon a rich and varied life, there is one thing I truly regret. One thing only that I wish could be undone: trying illegal drugs.

In my day, cannabis was hailed as the wonderdrug favoured by cool role-models like the Beatles and Rolling Stones. A gift of nature, mind-expanding, unlike the alcohol stupefying our parents at posh dinner-parties and violent drunkards beating their wives. We believed we were the ones who'd got it right.

I don't recall much else from that period, the flower-power summer of 1967. I'm hazily aware of some short-lived friendships, a subtle change of personality, and an increasingly idle existence.

I soon gave up experimenting, put off, I imagine, by the rapid intake of so-called friends into mental institutions after overtripping on LSD; and the arrest of some of them for possession and supply.

Months of inner chaos followed, turmoil, disarray. How much of this was due to herbal magic I shall never know. And that is what I most deplore.

With all its ups and downs, life holds one comfort: it's all exclusively our own, absorbed into our being, imprinting its unique design.

But this part wasn't me. Artificially induced, it forms a void in my consciousness. A big chunk stolen from my total life experience.

The earliest myths of many cultures are based on the theme of dispossession: the hero who, deprived of his heritage, fights endless battles to regain what is rightfully his.

So deeply ingrained is this preoccupation that, after thousands of years of human development, it remains a prime concern.

Of course, if we try, we can all imagine ourselves as dispossessed. In some respect, at some level, everyone can conceive a grievance over entitlements not provided.

It seems a significant portion of humanity go through life as self-appointed creditors, convinced that they have somehow been cheated out of their fair share. Envy, parsimony, greed – even theft, fraud and addiction – what are they if not attempts to redress the balance between the hand you've been dealt and the cards you consider owing?

The illusion of dispossession is often cultivated as a poor excuse for selfish and unscrupulous behaviour. Although few things could be less conducive to personal happiness.

It helps to be aware that we possess nothing by right. All we have - life itself – is ours by grace alone.

And how many times in the history of mankind will someone have received all he believed was his due?

Philosophers agree that human consciousness goes through different evolutionary stages:

We start as infants at the bottom of the pyramid, living by instinct and desire. No awareness of good and evil, right or wrong.

A lot of people never make it beyond this level. They go through life like self-motivated robots, eating, drinking, working, reproducing, without ever asking themselves why. Some make a right mess of their conditions: with nothing but primitive urges to guide you, it's easy to lose control.

At school-age we learn about discipline, about adjusting to a social system. We follow rules, adopt dogma, from authority or peers, to the point of fundamentalism. It's nice and secure to be told what to think, to be free of personal responsibility. That's why so many elect to stay within a closed system: blind adherents to religion, politics or ideology; to institutions or all-powerful employers, to convention and bigotry.

Those, however, who grow up to be individuals in their own right soon start to question other people's values, to criticize and evaluate. At levels of further education, sceptics and cynics abound. They do useful work as demolition contractors, but are less efficient at building things up.

Maturity comes when we liberate ourselves from the narrow scope of reaction. Go beyond the matter and acknowledge the infinite: the miracle of each existence; the deep significance of being alive.

Only when we arrive at this level of consciousness, say the philosophers, does life finally acquire some meaning.

Wisdom

Once upon a time in ancient China, a young man looked out one morning to find that a beautiful black mare had arrived in his father's field.

"Isn't that lucky?" he exclaimed. "I've always wanted a horse of my own!" But his wise old father warned him: "Good luck, bad luck – who knows?"

The lad rushed out to ride the mare, but promptly fell off and broke his leg. "Just my luck," he groaned. "Now that I finally have a horse I can't ride it!" The father reiterated: "Good luck, bad luck – who knows?"

Soon after the Emperor's envoy came to conscript all fit young men for the army. "So I was lucky after all," said the boy. "As a conscript I could have been killed." His father made his usual comment: "Good luck, bad luck – who knows?"

Indeed, when the village was regaled with tales of heroic deeds, glorious victories, the son cursed his broken leg and the ill-fated mare who'd caused it. The father had to remind him: "Good luck, bad luck – who knows?"

And when in due course word reached the village that all the young conscripts had been slaughtered in a skirmish...

This story can go on *ad infinitum*, for as long as it takes to convince us that things are rarely, if ever, quite as good or as bad as they appear.

"Good luck, bad luck – who knows?"

With new scientific methods to measure brain activity, it has now become possible to clinically define happiness.

Trials have shown that, in our culture, the cerebral rection we refer to as happiness occurs mainly in response to various stimulants: material, sexual, chemical...

However, such gratification soon wears off, making it necessary to renew the fix. Modern life is for many a restless chase for whatever it takes to make them feel better: pleasure as an occasionally induced, transitory state.

But the trials also revealed that certain brains seemed to be in a permanent state of bliss. In interviews these individuals confirmed that they did indeed consider themselves very fortunate.

And so another investigation commenced: the search for a single factor common to these people who, it appeared, held the key to constant happiness.

Interestingly, there was one point, on which they all concurred: Having devoted their lives to doing something worthwhile that they felt helped other people and society as a whole, they never doubted that they were needed, valued and appreciated.

The conclusion is so simple as to be almost embarrassing: To be happy ever after, with no need for a single stimulant, you only have to do one thing: Make yourself useful.

In every life, there are dead ends, points of little hope or vision, where we flounder aimlessly with no focus, no goal in sight. This is when depression is likely to set in, perhaps not without good reason. One school of thought regards depression as a form of spiritual guidance: a call from the deeper layers of ourselves that our life, or our attitude to it, needs attention.

On one such occasion in my past, someone suggested to me an image that has stayed with me ever since: of our days on earth being like so many gems, waiting to be picked off the ground, dull and raw, but each possessing a hidden beauty of its own.

Life then, is the string provided for threading these precious stones, one after another, to form a unique sequence. We are free to treat our gems as we see fit: leave them as they are, or cut and polish each one to perfection.

All are different, some brilliant and crystal clear, others richly opaque, a few dark and mysterious. But we only get the one chance to bring out the best in each stone, and once in place, it can never be changed, not without the chain breaking.

Like the gems, each day of life has its given place in the sequence, its inherent value to add to the rest. And whatever it takes, whatever it brings, it is worth taking care of.

"Each prison sentence is a sentence for life," a philosopher proclaimed. "No matter how many years of virtue precede it; no matter how impeccable your subsequent behaviour – in the eyes of the world you will always be an ex-convict. And this, maybe, for a single act, one mere instant of yielding to an impulse of destruction..."

But destructive behaviour rarely occurs out of the blue. Fuelled by bitterness, anger and resentment, it builds up gradually, insidiously, over a long period, to erupt eventually, often to the surprise of those around, who have failed to notice its slow, steady accumulation.

For while most of us are taught to differentiate between good and evil, we receive little instruction in recognizing destructive tendencies, and no guidance at all in handling the urge to annihilate whatever, whoever, threatens, hurts or annoys us.

No one is immune to these dangerous instincts. And unless we help each other control, not only our actions, but also our thinking, along constructive lines, any of us could fall victim to an impulsive act so devastating that it will mark us for the rest of our life.

It may not be the twist of a knife, the squeezing of a trigger, but something mundane, like pressing the accelerator a fraction too hard.

Sometimes a word will suffice to cause damage that nothing, no measure of good will, can ever repair.

If you went to see your doctor tomorrow and were diagnosed with a terminal illness, untreatable, incurable; giving you at best a few months to live... How do you think you would react?

Would you refuse to accept it? Stick your head in the sand and go on living as before, for as long as you were able? Or boldly abandon all routines, be a daredevil, travel round the world, spend your money, live life to the full?

Perhaps you would rather devote yourself fully to your family, making up for lost time? Do things you'd planned for your retirement? Or spend time on your own, contemplating your fore-shortened life, its inevitable outcome?

You might have issues to raise with yourself: knots that need untangling? The bitter venom of lingering resentment? Forgiveness outstanding, comfort withheld? Kindness casually suspended, help or support refused? Or even something as basic as love left unexpressed?

Since there is no guarantee for any life to extend beyond tomorrow, the best we can do is be prepared. Aim for the serenity that comes from treating each day as if it were the last.

Not only will it bring an improvement to our quality of life, while we have it; but also greatly diminish the fearsome sting of death.

Dreams

Hillwalking in Connemara, my guide stopped and pointed across a broad expanse of barren bogland.

Down there was a townland with a substantial two-storey house surrounded by mature trees, smooth green fields, solid stone walls: all testimony to erstwhile prosperity.

Apparently, this had not always prevailed. At one time, a man had lived there on his own, starving in a hovel, struggling to survive. Then one night he had a dream that, if he went to the bridge in Limerick, his fortune would be made.

With little to lose he set out, walking for days, until he found the bridge. He lingered there, but nothing happened. After three days, a man stopped and asked, what keeps you here, stranger?

Hearing about the dream, the Limerick man laughed out loud. "What would the world be like, if we all followed our dreams? I dreamt one night I was in a place called Úraid. I dug in a place between twin thorn trees and unearthed a pot of gold. But never would I be such a fool as to take any notice of that!"

"Thank you," said the man from Úraid and returned home, to dig in the spot between the twin thorn trees. The pot of gold was there; his fortune was made.

This is the place I call home: Where dreams take precedence.

Do you dream at night? According to brain scientists, everybody dreams, every single night, only one is not always aware of it.

The problem is, it happens all the time that we are claimed by our external reality the moment we wake up. Domestic, personal, professional concerns blot out whatever intriguing message the secret part of us was trying to convey.

For some it's a deliberate choice: restricting your existence to the surface may seem safer than exploring the murky depths underneath. But by persistently ignoring this path into the unconscious, you deprive yourself of a significant personal resource.

Living without your dreams is like struggling along myopic, without wearing your glasses. Put them on – and you'll see straight away the interesting nuances you've been missing.

Like a new perspective transcending your limited field of vision. A springboard to places where you've never been before. Insights beyond your normal perception, bordering on prophetic.

It's easy to nurture this link with your inner self. On waking up, keep your eyes closed, stay with your dreams until they have registered. Listen carefully, invite them on board – and then notice the difference when you take on the world.

All my adult life I've had the same recurring dream:

I am standing outside one of the houses where I used to live in the past, when I see a road, or a pathway, leading off to somewhere behind it.

Intrigued, I follow the path, walk along an avenue of flowering shrubs, into a village with cobbled streets, quaint architecture, cosy inns, pretty little shops: all very appealing.

Delighted to have found this perfect idyll, I am also filled with wonder that I have lived for so long in this place having no idea what lay behind it.

The feeling of elation persists when I wake up. It stays with me for days, fading away only gradually.

In recent times, I have deduced that this must be my sub-conscious mind pointing out that fulfilment would have been within reach, right there on my doorstep, if I had only taken the trouble to look for it.

For that is one important thing that I've learnt in life: If you don't expect to find it, you never notice the path to happiness, even if it's staring you in the face. My dream makes up for past neglect, instilling in my memory the joy that was lacking. The simple joys of life that are always there, waiting to be savoured.

I suppose it is a good sign that, with each year, my dream becomes less frequent. Even so, I miss it.

If you don't believe in prayers, make a wish instead. Every night, before you go to sleep, make a mental list of anything you wish for, ranging it in order of priority.

If nothing else, it will help establish in your own mind what, at this particular juncture, you consider most important. That alone is very useful information.

What is more, you may find that quite a few of these wishes – more, perhaps, than you'd expected – will actually come true.

It depends, of course, on the nature of each wish. The more sound and constructive your dreams and ambitions, the more likely they are to be realised.

A valid wish is more like an inspired insight into your current status quo and its most logical progression. You'll agree that in hindsight it's often apparent that most developments in life were probable, not to say inevitable, though at the time they happened they weren't seen as such.

The simple act of wishing can help us negotiate our passage though life. Enable us to weed out aspirations that are wasted, unrealistic or unworthy, and focus instead on refining the list until we find that most of our wishes are valid enough to be fulfilled.

Day dreams, pipe dreams, are usually dismissed as an escape, not altogether healthy, away from the realities of life. But dreams can also be the opposite: an escort to help you find your way home.

Make sure, though, that you're not misguided by false imaginings: of fame and fortune, eminence, promotion, wealth; phenomenal success of one kind or another. Such fantasies are often imposed by the world we live in, designed with the aim of reducing us all to robots.

The same goes for aspirations to comply with criteria prescribed by your peer group, suggesting that certain attributes like the right handbag, holiday, golf club, have a bearing on your personal value.

To qualify as the genuine article, a dream has to be of your own making: a genuine aspiration coming from within, uninfluenced by others. Look upon it as a statement of your individuality, your destiny made manifest.

Dream on, alone or with your partner. Pursue your ideal scenario. Visualize the future: your life at its best.

How it could be. How it will be. If you let it.

Goodness

Looking around, it is hard at times to believe that a thing like goodness, goodness for its own sake, exists. Where would it come from? What would its function be? Why would it be in evidence in some instances and not in others?

Do we carry it within us? Is it an innate characteristic, part of our natural heritage, although frequently obscured by self-oriented motives, promoted and condoned by a pragmatic tradition of each for himself?

Or does it reside elsewhere, beyond us, beyond our conscious comprehension? Is it something we have to go out and forage for? If so, how are we meant to go about it?

Anyone searching for goodness is bound to end up disillusioned. The opposite is so much easier to find. Who hasn't observed – perhaps even experienced – situations where yielding to the lower human instincts sends a character sliding swiftly and inevitably downhill?

But wait a minute! Does not this suggest that actions determine our integrity, rather than the other way round? And following on: that goodness does not appear out of the blue to perform bountiful deeds, but emerges as a result of the deeds themselves.

In other words: goodness has to be created. To convince ourselves of its existence, all we have to do is practice it.

"How can these things happen?" I asked a weathered professional soldier, who had been all over the world seeing evidence of more atrocities than most. "How does evil get such a hold as to make them possible?"

"Many go along with it out of fear," he replied. "Close their eyes rather than risk their life or that of loved ones."

"But the ones who instigate them?" I contended. "Are they never troubled by such a thing as conscience?"

He smiled reflectively and then he said: "I've come to the conclusion that there is no goodness inherent in the human race. Humanity is more like a fertile soil where anything can grow. Seeds of every kind abound, from the loveliest blossom to poisonous plants and weeds that choke everything in their path.

"Civilisation is the facility we have for turning our land into a beautiful garden. It tells us what's worth cultivating, what needs fertilizing or pruning, and what should be uprooted and destroyed.

"However, once you adopt a regime that, for reasons of its own, advocates or even tolerates the wrong kind of growth, it goes out of control very quickly, resulting in wilderness and, ultimately, a waste land.

"It has always happened and will happen, again and again, anytime, anywhere, if we as gardeners don't do our job of carefully tending what we've been given."

In his old age, my father-in-law went to commiserate and offer his help to a neighbour, who had been left paralysed after a stroke.

The man, a retired Brigadier, had devoted his retirement to running a soldiers' charity. Now he had one favour to ask: "If you were to take over as President of the organisation, it would put my mind at rest."

"No," said my father-in-law, "that's not the way we'll do it. I shall gladly do the work, for which you're no longer able. But you will remain in your position. I'll act as your deputy, taking instructions from you."

It was the Brigadier's wife who told me the story, years after they'd both passed away.

"Thanks to this arrangement," she said, "my husband lived on for another six years. It made him feel he was still needed. He still had much to give. All the while, his friend worked tirelessly on his behalf, accepting no recognition for his efforts, ensuring all credit went to the President."

Aware, no doubt, that it was a fact he himself would never have acknowledged, she declared: "Your father-in-law was a very good man."

Towards the end of his life, he had said to me: "When I think of all the unhappiness I have witnessed over eight decades, it brings me to the conclusion that every form of misery in the world is caused by one single human failing:

Selfishness."

Sometimes, when my little boy asked me to explain an unusual word or concept that was hard to describe succinctly, I would simply quote the opposite: "It's something that is not such-and-such."

In the same way, I find there are occasions when goodness cannot be fully appreciated without the antipode of evil being there to define it.

Perhaps the only way to live with the knowledge of intolerable evil deeds taking place all around, is by seeing them as an inevitable component of human life, without which we could never tell what's good and what isn't.

Those who fall victim to the evil acts of others ought to be revered as martyrs sacrificed on our behalf, so that goodness can continue to live amongst us.

For their loved ones one can only hope that the heartfelt sympathy brought out by such tragic events will offer some small comfort.

The fact that it is inescapable does not mean that evil should be tolerated. On the contrary, it should be fought continually, in all its forms, on all levels: in parliaments and courtrooms, in media, schools and homes, and, of course primarily, within ourselves.

Hating evil will clear the way to goodness. Fighting it makes us good. Just as tolerating it makes us, to some extent, evil.

I'd come a long way to visit my grandparents' grave. As I was planting an aquilegia, my grandmother's favourite flower, a man in a dog-collar came up, introducing himself as the new vicar.

I told him that my first home had been with the encumbents of this grave. Nodding kindly, absent-mindedly, he said he must be on his way. "A pleasure meeting you. Nice to think that you're still here."

I smiled politely in reply, inwardly shattered by the idea that I should never have left this place. Even at the age of four, standing by the hall window to see the express train from Paris to Oslo halt for custom clearance, I would watch the continental travellers: elegant, worldly, exciting, stretching their legs along the platform; and dream of the day when I would be one of them.

Still – standing here now, in front of the memorial raised over those two who gave me the most precious heritage I possess, I am aware that one part of me did in fact remain here.

It was buried in my grandparents' grave, not to decay and perish, but to take root, along with the memory of their goodness; grow strong and viable in the black earth, blossom like the aquilegia, and bear fruit ever after.

Nature

"I don't look upon it as a special gift," said the young woman, who's made a name for herself for her ability to communicate with animals. "To me it's the most natural thing in the world."

Having closeted herself with my aged dog, she brought back a piece of information that only the dog could have supplied, together with a message that proved very helpful.

She explained that her mode of communication was entirely non-verbal: mental images she sent out and received by way of reply.

One day she'd been called to a house where an owl had settled into the garage. The owner had tried, time and again, to return the bird to the wild, but it kept reappearing.

"It's not that I mind her being there," he said. "But it's not much of a life for an owl, is it? Could you please do your best to find out why she won't leave?"

A session with the owl left the woman perplexed. Apparently, the attraction of the garage was a chance to move through the air at speed, with no flapping of wings.

On receiving this message, the man laughed and said it made perfect sense. "Every time I go out on my motor-bike, she comes along, sitting on my shoulder. I can tell how much she loves it."

"So he didn't really need me at all," the woman concluded. "With animals it's often enough to trust your instincts."

I've never doubted that genes have a memory, since the day when I uncoiled, with a hissing sound, a new, bright green garden hose across my stable-yard.

The four Connemara ponies, normally so placid, fearless as they come, went into hysterics. From their reactions you'd have thought that a deadly giant green mamba had suddenly been released amongst them.

But why were they afraid? They were Irish-bred ponies, they could have no acquired recollection of snakes. We haven't had snakes in Ireland since they were banished by St. Patrick.

Their panic could only have been caused by some inbred warning mechanism left over from their wild ancestors, who depended on it for survival on the steppes of Inner Asia thousands of years ago.

A recent BBC documentary hailed a revolutionary scientific breakthrough: the discovery of genetic memory. Extensive tests had confirmed that inherited characteristics could be affected by the experiences of previous generations.

But we don't need scientists to tell us that. To be aware that we carry within us the heritage of those who went before: the imprint of their dreams and aspirations, triumphs and achievements, traumas and despair, all we have to do is look deeply into our own heart.

The three-year-old I was minding, a quiet lad of few words, had come along to help me feed the ponies.

Filling buckets in the tack-room, I noticed him staring, deep in thought, at a mouldy rein hanging from a rusty nail: a remnant left by a former occupier.

"My horse was Jacky," he uttered vacantly. I straightened up. "What did you say?" He looked at me, slightly bashful, as if he'd spoken out of turn. "I had a horse called Jacky."

"When was that?" I asked gently. "Oh…" His gaze lost itself in the distance. "It was a long long time ago."

I was anxious to hear more, all about Jacky, but the boy had no more to offer. "I can't remember. It's gone."

I've noticed that mystical experiences such as this are often connected with animals. Perhaps they form our one remaining link with the natural world inhabited by our ancestors before it was discarded in favour of our present materially oriented sphere.

One thing that amazes me about the 2004 tsanumi, is that so few animals perished. From rats to elephants, they had the good sense to escape in time to the safety of higher ground. Only the humans remained on the beach: swimming, sunbathing, having fun; oblivious to the imminent mortal danger.

What has the human race done to deprive itself of a life-saving faculty accessible even to a rat?

I've had my share of inexplicable experiences: telepathic communications, synchronicities, prophetic dreams, appearances of ghosts, even the banshee.

In the past I kept very quiet about these things, but I don't any more. I like to discuss them, hear other people's comments.

The most common is a dry dismissal: "You're obviously very psychic." But I don't think so. I believe we are all in possession of the same sixth sense, though many lack access to it.

This no doubt is due to the culture we have created: a culture dedicated to reducing human life to one single, easily managed, easily understood dimension.

Once the mind has barricaded itself against anything but rational thought, blocking off the conduits with sceptical and cynical debris, it will have great difficulty receiving and processing esoteric information.

A deepset fear of the unknown may also be behind the vehemence with which the mystical, incomprehensible is routinely renounced and rejected.

Others, like me, see a promise of hope and comfort in the prospect of a realm beyond sense and senses.

The one thing to terrify me would be the aimless spectacle, the howling emptiness of a life extending no further than the paltry limitations of the material world.

When Muffin, my terrier, died aged sixteen, I lost a trusty companion who had shared a major part of my adult life. The void she left was greater than I'd expected.

The first morning without her, on waking up, I had a vision of a summer meadow. In amongst the flowers and tall grass, was Muffin, no longer old and decrepit, but full of the joys of spring, running around in leaps and bounds, as she hadn't done since she was a puppy.

The image of her, so happy and carefree, stayed with me all day. It made me feel much better.

The following morning, the same meadow appeared in my mind's eye. Muffin was running along the far edge, on her way out of the picture. She kept glancing anxiously towards me, the way she used to when seeking my approval.

It's all right, Muffin, I thought sleepily. You go on, if you have to, I wouldn't want to hold you back. We had a great time together, but all things come to an end. And I have my memories to sustain me.

The third morning: the meadow once more. As lovely as ever – but no sign of a dog.

Whenever in future I have to face bereavement, I shall remember the sunlit meadow: the message it contained.

Death

In failing health, my mother-in-law declared that she would select for herself a suitable resting-place. So one fine Sunday we set out in her car for a tour of Connemara graveyards.

The one she chose was tucked away on the strand beneath an ancient church ruin overlooking a turquoise lagoon.

In return for a bottle of Paddy's whiskey and a homemade fruitcake specially brought for the purpose, the caretaker promised to reserve the best plot: 'the one with the fairest view'.

Having marked it out with breeze blocks, we picnicked by her future grave, enjoying the peace and the beauty of this wild, remote spot. "I don't mind at all," she said, sipping her coffee, "ending my days on earth, if it's in a place like this. Except for the fact that I shall be all alone."

She was delighted when I vowed that I'd be buried next to her, and that she wouldn't have to wait long. After all, what was forty or fifty years in the face of eternity?

Only a few months later, on a stormy October day, I was back to see her coffin lowered into the ground. I thought of our picnic, and the warmth of that moment took much of my sadness away.

We go and see her now and then. And while children and dogs play on the strand, I draw a peculiar comfort from the fact that I am visiting my own grave.

I know of someone who was diagnosed with a terminal illness. A man in his prime, happily married, with a young family.

"This isn't possible," was his reaction. "I can't die now. I have too much undone." And he sat down and made a list of all the things he wanted to accomplish before departing from this life.

The doctors were amazed to see the improvement in his health, as he worked his way through the items, ticking them off one by one.

"The question isn't whether or not you live," he told me, smiling, on one occasion. "What matters is how, and why."

In due course the inevitable happened: he reached the end of his list. The illness returned. Within weeks he had left us, passed away peacefully.

His story makes me wonder: is this how it is for everybody? Do we all have our set agenda, and when we get to the end of it, our life is over?

This man was privileged. He made up his own list. Most of us have it written for us, with little say in the matter.

We don't even get to read it, and only a chosen few know when we've reached the end.

A member of my extended family was killed in an accident, aged twenty.

How can you come to terms with that? How can his parents be expected ever to come to terms with it? All those years of caring and nurturing, seeing him grow and learn – what were they for?

The only comfort I could find was the thought that perhaps he wasn't meant to live longer. His life span, we now know, measured twenty years. We shouldn't look upon it against the possibility that it might have been much longer, but accept the gift of those years and value them accordingly.

"How do I know that I will survive?" asked my young son after learning about his cousin's death. "You probably will," I reassured him. "These days in Ireland, most children do survive. But no one can be completely certain, and that is how it has to be. Because if we could take for granted that everyone lives to a ripe old age, we wouldn't take good enough care of each other."

As I said it, my heart went out to those parents who have to pay the price for that precious uncertainty.

Let us never forget their pain, the cross they carry on behalf of those more fortunate.

On a visit to my native Sweden, I read a death notice in the paper: An old friend of mine had lost her mother.

'*The funeral has taken place*,' it said. I was disappointed. I would have liked to pay my last respects to this kindly woman who had often welcomed me into her home.

A few days later, when I rang up to offer my condolences, my friend gave a cool response. She seemed, if anything, embarrassed. As if death and grief were something shameful: the ultimate social failure.

It transpired she had just come back from the funeral. The statement in the paper had been incorrect, printed deliberately to discourage fellow-mourners turning up. "I mean, who'd want to be sociable on an occasion like that?"

My thoughts went to funerals at home in Connemara: long motorcades escorting the hearse, wakes lasting through the night, endless tokens of comfort and sympathy.

And I imagined the lonely figure of my Swedish friend hunched in a pew in a near-empty church, harbouring the grief that she wouldn't, or couldn't, allow anyone to share.

How lucky we are in rural Ireland, where death is still regarded as an integral part of life. The one thing we all have in common and endure together in the sombre knowledge that no one is spared.

When I was nineteen, I was seriously injured in a car crash. In fact, I very nearly died.

I remember that night following surgery. Like many patients in a critical condition, I found myself passing through a long tunnel: like being born all over again. As at birth, a light beckoned at the end, infinitely alluring.

I would have reached it, had it not been for the intervention of three nurses. Three young women whom I'd never seen before and would never see again. I recall to this day their eager, youthful faces, the tears in their eyes as they pleaded with me to remain in this world a little while longer.

Sartre used to say: hell is other people. I disagree. Life is other people. Those nameless young nurses were speaking, not for themselves but for others: Their plea was on behalf of the husband, the child I would once have, and of any other person to whom my continued existence would possibly one day make a difference.

It was for them I came back, for all they had to offer me, for all I had to offer them: a decision I've never regretted.

There are times when I long to return to the stillness and peace of that dark tunnel, the reassuring light shining at the end. But I know it will still be there for me when the day comes.

I'm in no hurry.

O

is a symbol of the world,
of oneness and unity. O Books
explores the many paths of wholeness
and spiritual understanding which
different traditions have developed down
the ages. It aims to bring this knowledge
in accessible form, to a general readership,
providing practical spirituality to today's seekers.

For the full list of over 200 titles covering:

- CHILDREN'S PRAYER, NOVELTY AND GIFT BOOKS
- CHILDREN'S CHRISTIAN AND SPIRITUALITY
- CHRISTMAS AND EASTER
- RELIGION/PHILOSOPHY
- SCHOOL TITLES
- ANGELS/CHANNELLING
- HEALING/MEDITATION
- SELF-HELP/RELATIONSHIPS
- ASTROLOGY/NUMEROLOGY
- SPIRITUAL ENQUIRY
- CHRISTIANITY, EVANGELICAL
  AND LIBERAL/RADICAL
- CURRENT AFFAIRS
- HISTORY/BIOGRAPHY
- INSPIRATIONAL/DEVOTIONAL
- WORLD RELIGIONS/INTERFAITH
- BIOGRAPHY AND FICTION
- BIBLE AND REFERENCE
- SCIENCE/PSYCHOLOGY

Please visit our website,
www.O-books.net

SOME RECENT O BOOKS

Aim for the Stars...Reach the Moon

How to coach your life to spiritual and material success

Conor Patterson

A fascinating, intelligent, and beneficial tool and method of programming your mind for success. The techniques are fast to achieve, motivating, and inspiring. I highly recommend this book. Uri Geller

1905047274 208pp £11.99 $19.95

Amulets

Kim Farnell

This is a wonderful book for those interested in learning about amulets and how to create them. Farnell's expertise makes her the ideal guide. Her knowledge is sound and her instructions are always clear and easy to follow. The strength of this book lies in it being one of easy access and also very well presented in its structure and internal logic. It makes an ideal reference book for anyone of a serious interest, being equally suited to beginners and experts alike. Deborah Houlding, author of *The Houses: Temples of the Sky*

1846940060 160pp £9.99 $14.95

Developing Spiritual Intelligence

The power of you

Altazar Rossiter

This beautifully clear and fascinating book is an incredibly simple guide to that which so many of us search for: the kind of spiritual intelligence that

will enable us to live peacefully, intelligently, and joyfully whatever our circumstances. It brings the spiritual world down to earth, which is just where we need it to be in order to take our next step. Dr Dina Glouberman author of Life Choices, Life Changes and co-founder of Skyros
1905047649 240pp £12.99 $19.95

God Calling
A Devotional Diary
A. J. Russell
46th printing
Perhaps the best-selling devotional book of all time, over 6 million copies sold.
1905047428 280pp 135/95mm £7.99 cl.
US rights sold

Happiness in 10 Minutes
Brian Mountford
Brian Mountford-in exploring "happiness"-celebrates the paradox of losing and finding at its heart. At once both profound and simple, the book teaches us that to be fully alive is to be in communion and that gratitude leads us into the mystery of giving ourselves away-the path of true joy. Alan Jones, Dean of Grace Cathedral, San Francisco, author of Reimagining Christianity.
1905047770 128pp b/w illustrations £6.99 $9.95

Head Versus Heart-and our Gut Reactions

The 21st century enneagram

Michael Hampson

A seminal work, whose impact will continue to reverberate throughout the 21st century because of two original contributions. Firstly, Hampson provides a credible, coherent and compelling explanation of the inter relationships between the nine categories of the Enneagram recast as the Strategy Board. Secondly, he has generalised the Enneagram so that it can be used as a tool of analysis in many fields of human endeavour, bringing illumination and allowing insights to tumble out. Fr Alexander, Worth Abbey

19038169000 320pp £11.99 $16.95

I Am With You

The best-selling modern inspirational classic

John Woolley

14th printing hardback

Probably the consistently best-selling devotional in the UK today.

0853053413 280pp 150x100mm £9.99 cl

4th printing paperback

1903816998 280pp 150/100mm £6.99 $12.95

Souls Don't Lie

A true story of past lives

Jenny Smedley

People often go on about past lives they believe they've had, but rarely has

anyone explained so eloquently and succinctly the art and science of using past-life regression to heal the life you're living now - a fascinating and recommended read. Barefoot Doctor, healer and author.
1905047835 224pp £11.99 $19.95

The 7 Ahas! of Highly Enlightened Souls
How to free yourself from ALL forms of stress
Mike George

7th printing

A very profound, self empowering book. Each page bursting with wisdom and insight. One you will need to read and reread over and over again! Paradigm Shift
1903816319 128pp 190/135mm £5.99 $11.95

The 9 Dimensions of the Soul
Essence and the Enneagram
David Hey

The first book to relate the two, understanding the personality types of the Enneagram in relation to the Essence. In doing so it sheds a new light on our personality, its origins and how it operates, presenting an accurate map of our inner and outer self, our personality and our inner being. The Nine Dimensions of the Soul *is written in a beautifully simple, insightful and heartful way and transmits complex material in a way that is easy to read and understand.* Thomas O. Trobe, MD Psychiatrist and Founder and Director of Learning Love Seminars, Inc.
1846940028 160pp £10.99 $19.95

The Barefoot Indian

Julia Heywood

Spiritual fiction, or not? Eternal wisdom is expressed in the context of modern day to day life, in a fresh, sensitive, intuitive, humorous and profoundly inspirational way.

1846940400 196pp £9.99 $19.95

The Goddess, the Grail and the Lodge

The Da Vinci code and the real origins of religion

Alan Butler

5th printing

This book rings through with the integrity of sharing time-honoured revelations. As a historical detective, following a golden thread from the great Megalithic cultures, Alan Butler vividly presents a compelling picture of the fight for life of a great secret and one that we simply can't afford to ignore. From the foreword by Lynn Picknett & Clive Prince

1903816696 360pp 230/152mm £12.99 $19.95

The Heart of Tantric Sex

A sourcebook on the practice of Tantric sex

Diana Richardson

3rd printing

One of the most revolutionary books on sexuality ever written. Ruth Ostrow, News Ltd.

1903816378 256pp £9.99 $14.95

The Quest

Exploring a sense of soul

Dawes, Dolley and Isaksen

This remarkable course draws on a wide variety of psychospiritual approaches. The intent is to guide readers on the spiritual journey in a way that enables them to find their own answers through reflection and practical exercises. This is not another hyped up DIY book but rather a carefully considered and comprehensive guide to psychospiritual development. There is an invaluable resource list at the back. Scientific and Medical Network Review

1903816939 264pp £9.99 $16.95

The Soulbane Illusion

Norman Jetmundsen

Truly great writing...I was inspired. It is something I can recommend to anyone interested in the supernatural/thriller with a foundational faith to inspire people. If you like the works of C S Lewis, you will like this; if you like the works of John Grisham, you will like this. A good blend of the two. Roundtable Review

1903816599 308pp £7.99 $12.95

The Soulbane Stratagem

Norman Jetmundsen

2nd printing

Listed by Wesley Owen as one of the all-time top 10 great Christian fiction titles. Rewarding, perhaps even life-changing; a readable, spiritually instructive work which should find a wide market. The Anniston Star

1903019699 296pp £6.99 $12.95

The Tree That Talked

Jenny Smedley

The 300 year story of an acorn to an oak, and the life around it.

1846940354 160pp £10.99 $16.95

Torn Clouds

A time-slip novel of reincarnation and romance, threaded through with the myths and magic of ancient Egypt.

Judy Hall

This is a great novel. It has suspense, drama, coincidence, and an extra helping of intrigue. I would recommend this literary marvel to anyone drawn to the magic, mystery and exotic elegance known as Egypt. Planet Starz

1903816807 400pp £9.99 $14.95

Zen Economics

Save the world and yourself by saving

Robert van de Weyer

This book carries several messages of hope, which are linked by the theme of saving and investing. Its single most important message is that in the western world most of us have reached a point of prosperity where the investment with the highest rate of return is investing in the self.

1903816785 96pp £6.99 $14.95